OCR GCSE

Religious Studies A
World Religion(s)

Judaism

Janet Green · Cavan Wood

Series editor: Janet Dyson
Series consultant: Jon Mayled

OCR

RECOGNISING ACHIEVEMENT | Heinemann

Official Publisher Partnership

OCR AND HEINEMANN ARE WORKING TOGETHER TO PROVIDE BETTER SUPPORT FOR YOU

GW01072049

Heinemann is an imprint of Pearson Education Limited, a company incorporated in England and Wales, having its registered office at Edinburgh Gate, Harlow, Essex, CM20 2JE. Registered company number: 872828

www.heinemann.co.uk

Heinemann is a registered trademark of Pearson Education Limited

Text © Pearson Education Limited 2009

First published 2009

13 12 11 10 09

10 9 8 7 6 5 4 3 2 1

British Library Cataloguing in Publication Data
A catalogue record for this book is available from the British Library

ISBN 978 0 435 50133 4

Edited by Bruce Nicholson and Leah Morin
Reviewed by Richard Gray
Proofread by Tracey Smith
Project managed and typeset by Wearset Ltd, Boldon, Tyne and Wear
Original illustrations © Pearson Education 2009
Illustrated by NB Illustration
Picture research by Q2AMedia
Cover photo/illustration © JUPITERIMAGES/Comstock Images/Alamy
Printed in Italy by Rotolito Lombarda S.p.A.

Acknowledgements
The author and publisher would like to thank the following individuals and organisations for permission to reproduce photographs:

p2 Nano/Istockphoto, p6 Galushko Sergey/Shutterstock, p8 Nort/Istockphoto, p12 Mikhail Pogosov/Shutterstock, p14 Time & Life Pictures/Getty Images, p16 Martin Gray/National Geographic/Getty Images, p18 Corbis, p26 Paul Prescott/Shutterstock, p28 Armonn/Dreamstime, p29 Tatiana Popova/Shutterstock, p30 Najlah Feanny/Corbis, p32 Eckehard Schulz/Associated Press, p34 TC. Kurt Holter/Shutterstock, p34 BHoward Sandler/Shutterstock, p38 Gil Cohen Magen/Reuters, p40 Muhammed Muheisen/Associated Press, p42 Roman Sigaev/BigStockPhoto, p44 Nextrecord/Fotolia, p46 Czardases/Istockphoto, p48 Philip Scalia/Alamy, p51 Time Life Pictures/Stringer/Getty Images, p56 Shai Ginott/Corbis, p60 Mikhail Levit/Shutterstock, p61 Ricki Rosen/Corbis Saba, p62 Lebrecht Music & Arts Photo Library/Photolibrary, p63 Ted Spiegel/Corbis, p64 Philip Lange/Shutterstock, p65 Helene Rogers/Art Directors & Trip Photo Library, p66 Rex Features, p67 Blaine Harrington III/Alamy, p68 Ted Spiegel/Corbis, p73 Kevin Frayer/Associated Press, p74 Hulton-Deutsch Collection/Corbis, p75 Gemma Levine/Contributor/Hulton Archive/Getty Images, p76 Photogl/Shutterstock, p82 Anyka/Shutterstock, p86 Manfred Steinbach/Shutterstock, p88 Martin D. Vonka/Shutterstock, p89 Chhobi/Dreamstime, p90 Abbarich/Dreamstime, p92 Alvaro Pantoja/Shutterstock, p94 Andy Aitchison/Corbis, p96 Irabassi's/Istockphoto, p97 Ben Dalfen, p98 Franka Bruns/Associated Press, p100 Global Photo/Istockphoto, p101 Israel images/Alamy, p107M Helene Rogers/Art Directors & Trip Photo Library, p107B Robert Mulder/Godong/Corbis, p107 T Baz Ratner/Associated Press, p110 Annie Griffiths Belt/Corbis, p112 Ted Spiegel/Corbis, p114 Comstock/Jupiter Images, p116 Adina Tovy/Art Directors & Trip Photo Library, p118 Israelimages/Brian Hendler, p120 Israel images/Alamy, p124 Philip Gould/Corbis, p128 Jupiter Images, p138 Christine Osborne/World Religions Photo Library, p139 Hannibal Hanschke/Reuters, 140 Des E Gershon/Alamy, p141 Efi Keren Photography/Photographersdirect, p144 vadim kozlovsky/Shutterstock, p145 Hulton Archive/Stringer/Getty Images, p146 Howard Sandler/Shutterstock, p149 Kathy Willens/Associated Press

All quotations reprinted from Tanakh: The Holy Scriptures: The new JPS Translation to the traditional Hebrew text © 1985 by The Jewish Publication Society, with the permission of the publisher.

Contents

Introduction

A note for teachers

This student book has been written especially to support the OCR Religious Studies Specification A, Units B579: *Judaism 1* (Core beliefs, Special days and pilgrimage, Major divisions and interpretations) and B580: *Judaism 2* (Places and forms of worship, Religion in the faith community and the family, Sacred writings). It is part of an overall series covering the OCR Specification A and comprising:

- a series of Student Books covering Christianity, Christianity from a Roman Catholic Perspective, Islam, Judaism and Perspectives on Christian Ethics – further details on pages viii and ix.
- a series of Teacher Guides: one covering Christianity, Islam and Judaism, and another three covering Buddhism, Hinduism and Sikhism – further details on page pages viii and ix.

Who are we?

The people who have planned and contributed to this series of books include teachers, advisers, inspectors, teacher trainers and GCSE examiners, all of whom have specialist knowledge of Religious Studies. For all of us the subject has a real fascination and we believe that good Religious Studies can make a major contribution to developing the skills, insights and understanding people need in today's world. In the initial development of this series, Pamela Draycott lent us her expertise, which we gratefully acknowledge.

Why is Religious Studies an important subject?

We believe that Religious Studies is an important subject because every area of life is touched by issues to do with religion and belief. Following a Religious Studies GCSE course will enable students to study and explore what people believe about God, authority, worship, beliefs, values and truth. Students will have opportunities to engage with questions about why people believe in God and how beliefs can influence many aspects of their lives.

Students will also explore why members of a particular religion may believe different things. In lessons students will be expected to think, talk, discuss, question and challenge, reflect on and assess a wide range of questions. As young people growing up in a diverse society studying religion will help them to understand and relate to people whose beliefs, values and viewpoints differ from their own, and help them to deal with issues arising, not only in school, but in the community and workplace.

The study of religion will also help students to make connections with a whole range of other important areas, such as music, literature, art, politics, economics and social issues.

The specification for OCR A Judaism

The specification outlines the aims and purposes of GCSE and the content to be covered is divided into six different Topics. The book's structure follows these Topic divisions precisely:

Topic 1: Core beliefs

Topic 2: Special days and pilgrimage

Topic 3: Major divisions and interpretations

Topic 4: Places and forms of worship

Topic 5: Religion in the faith community and the family

Topic 6: Sacred writings

The Topics focus on developing skills such as analysis, empathy and evaluation, which will enable students to gain knowledge and understanding of the specified content.

In following this specification students will have the opportunity to study Judaism in depth and will learn about the diversity of the faith and the way in which people who believe in the religion follow its teachings in their everyday lives.

This book covers everything students will need to know for the examination and shows them how to use their knowledge and understanding to answer the questions they will be asked.

Changes to the specification

The specification has changed dramatically according to the developing nature of education and the need to meet the demands of the world for students. The new specification will be taught from September 2009 onwards. The main changes that teachers and students should be aware of include the following:

- The Assessment Objectives (AOs) have changed, with a 50% focus now given to AO1 (Describe, explain and analyse, using knowledge and understanding) and a 50% focus to AO2 (Use evidence and reasoned argument to express and evaluate personal responses, informed insights and differing viewpoints). Previously, the balance was 75% to 25% respectively. There is more information on this on pages x and xi.

- There is an increased focus on learning *from* religion rather than simply learning *about* religion, and explicit reference to religious beliefs is now required in answers marked by Levels of Response.

- Levels of Response grids have been changed to a new range of 0 to 6 marks for AO1 questions and 0–12 marks for AO2 questions. See pages x and xi for the complete grids.

- Quality of Written Communication (QWC) is now only assessed on parts (d) and (e) of each question.

- Beyond the six Judaism Topics covered by this book, there is now a greater choice of Topics within the specification including a new Christian Scriptures paper on the Gospels of Mark and Luke, a paper on Muslim texts and a paper on Jewish texts.

- There is also more freedom to study different combinations of religions and Topics.

Why did we want to write these resources?

We feel strongly that there is a need for good classroom resources, which take advantage of the changed Assessment Objectives, and which:

- make the subject lively, interactive and relevant to today's world

- encourage students to talk to each other and work together

- challenge students and encourage them to think in depth in order to reach a high level of critical thinking

- train students to organise their thoughts in writing in a persuasive and structured way, and so prepare them for examination.

The book has many features which contribute towards these goals. **Grade Studio** provides stimulating and realistic exercises to train students in what examiners are looking for and how to meet those expectations. **Exam Café** provides an exciting environment in which students can plan and carry out their revision.

Of course learning is about more than just exams. Throughout the book you will find **Research Notes**, which encourage students to explore beyond the book and beyond the curriculum. All of these features are explained in more detail on the next two pages.

What is in this book?

This student book has the following sections;

- the **Introduction**, which you are reading now
- the six **Topics** covered in the specification
- **Exam Café** – an invaluable resource for students studying their GCSE in Religious Studies
- **Glossary** – a reference tool for key terms and words used throughout the book.

Each of the above is covered in more detail in the text below.

The six Topics

Each Topic in this book contains:

- a Topic scene-setter (**The Big Picture**)
- a look at the key questions raised by the Topic, and the key words and issues associated with those questions (**Develop your knowledge**)
- two-page spreads covering the **main Topic content**
- two pages of different level questions to check understanding of the Topic material (**Remember and Reflect**)
- exam-style questions with level indicators, examiner's comments and model answers (**Grade Studio**).

These features, which are explained more fully in the following pages, have been carefully planned and designed to draw together the OCR specification in an exciting but manageable way.

The Big Picture

This provides an overview of the Topic. It explains to students **what** they will be studying (the content), **how** they will study it (the approaches, activities and tasks) and

why they are studying it (the rationale). It also includes a **Get started** activity, often linked to a picture or visual stimulus, which presents a task designed to engage students in the issues of the Topic and give them some idea of the content to be studied.

Develop your knowledge

This lists the **key information**, **key questions** and **key words** of the Topic. At a glance, it allows students to grasp the basic elements of knowledge they will gain in the study of the Topic. It is also a useful reference point for reflection and checking information as it is studied.

Main Topic content

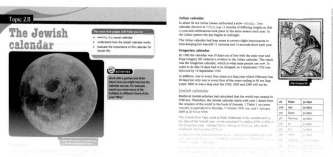

The main content of each Topic is covered in a number of two-page spreads. Each spread equates to roughly one lesson of work – although teachers will need to judge for themselves if some of these need more time.

Each spread begins with the **learning outcomes**, highlighted in a box at the top of the page, so that students are aware of the focus and aims of the lesson. The text then attempts to answer, through a balanced viewpoint, one or two of the key questions raised in

Develop your knowledge. The text carefully covers the views of both religious believers and non-believers. It is also punctuated with activities that range from simple tasks that can take place in the classroom to more complex tasks that can be tackled away from school.

A range of margin features adds extra depth and support to the main text both for students and the teacher.

- **For debate** invites students to examine two sides of a controversial issue.
- **Must think about!** directs students towards a key idea that they should consider.
- **Sacred text** provides an extract from the sacred texts of the religion to help students understand religious ideas and teachings.
- **Research notes** provides stimulating ideas for further research beyond the material covered in the book and in the OCR specification.

Activities

Every Topic has a range of interesting activities which will help students to achieve the learning outcomes. Every two-page spread has a short starter activity to grab students' attention and to get them thinking (see **Get Started** activity on page vi). This is followed by a development section where the main content is introduced, and a plenary activity, which may ask students to reflect on what they have learnt, or may start them thinking about the next steps.

All activities are labelled AO1 or AO2 so you can tell at a glance which skills will be developed.

Remember and Reflect

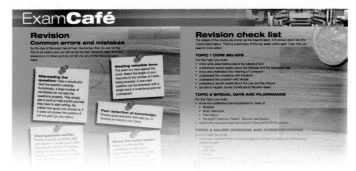

This provides an opportunity for students to reflect on what they have learned and identify possible weaknesses or gaps in their knowledge. It also helps them to recognise key ideas in the specification content. Once they have tested their knowledge with the first set of questions, a cross-reference takes them back to the relevant part of the text so they can check their answers. A second set of questions helps them to develop the AO2 skills necessary for the examination.

What is Grade Studio?

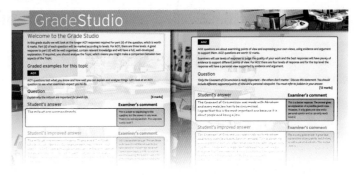

Everyone has different learning needs and this section of the book gives clear focus on how, with guidance from the teacher, students can develop the skills that will help them to achieve the higher levels in their exam responses.

Grade Studio appears as boxes within each Topic, as well as a two-page spread at the end of every Topic. It includes tips from the examiner, guidance on the steps to completing a well structured answer, and sample answers with examiner comments.

What is the Exam Café?

This is the revision section of the book. Here students will find useful revision tools and tips on how to get started on their revision and exam preparation. Students will also find assessment advice, including examples of different types of questions and samples of frequently asked questions. A useful **revision check list** allows students to review each Topic's content and explains where to find material in the book that relates to the exam questions.

Exam Café also has:

- sample student answers with examiner's comments
- help on understanding exam language, so students can achieve higher grades
- examiner tips, including common mistakes to be avoided.

Heinemann's OCR Religious Studies A Series

Below is a snapshot of the complete OCR Religious Studies A series. Further detail can be found at www.heinemann.co.uk/gcse

OCR A Teacher Guide – Christianity, Islam and Judaism, with editable CD-ROM

ISBN 978-0-435-50136-5

This Teacher Guide covers Christianity, Islam and Judaism. It corresponds throughout to the Student Books and contains lesson plans, worksheets and Grade Studios to provide a complete teaching course for the chosen religion(s). The Christianity section of the Teacher Guide covers each Topic in the specification with six sample lesson plans and worksheets. The other religions have three sample lesson plans and worksheets. Everything is cross-referenced to the student books to help you make the most out of these resources.

The Teacher Guide comes with an editable CD-ROM, which contains all the lesson plans along with a fully customisable version of all the worksheets.

Perspectives on Christian Ethics Student Book

ISBN 978-0-435-50270-6

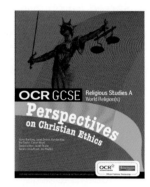

This book provides complete coverage of both units of Christian Ethics (B589 and B603). It provides information, activities, and Grade Studio examples for all aspects of the course, as well as an 8-page Exam Café for revision. Teachers will find support for almost all aspects of this course in the OCR B Teacher Guide: Philosophy and Applied Ethics (ISBN 978-0-435-50152-5).

Christianity Student Book

ISBN 978-0-435-50130-3

This book provides complete coverage of both units of Christianity (B571 and B572). It provides information, activities, and Grade Studio examples for all aspects of the course, as well as an 8-page Exam Café for revision. Comprehensive support for the Teacher is provided through the corresponding OCR A Teacher Guide (see above).

Islam Student Book

ISBN 978-0-435-50134-1

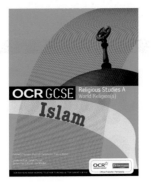

This book provides complete coverage of both units of Islam (B577 and B578). It provides information, activities, and Grade Studio examples for all aspects of the course, as well as an 8-page Exam Café for revision. Comprehensive support for the Teacher is provided through the corresponding OCR A Teacher Guide (see opposite).

Roman Catholic Student Book

ISBN 978-0-435-50132-7

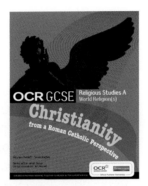

This book provides complete coverage of both units of Christianity (Roman Catholic) (B573 and B574). It provides information, activities, and Grade Studio examples for all aspects of the course, as well as an 8-page Exam Café for revision.

OCR A Teacher Guide – Buddhism

ISBN 978-0-435-50129-7

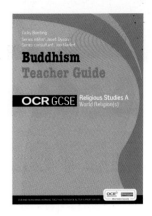

This Teacher Guide covers Buddhism. It contains lesson plans, worksheets and Grade Studios to provide a complete teaching course for Buddhism. It covers Units B569 and B570 in the OCR A specification.

OCR A Teacher Guide – Hinduism

ISBN 978-0-435-50128-0

This Teacher Guide covers Hinduism. It contains lesson plans, worksheets and Grade Studios to provide a complete teaching course for Hinduism. It covers Units B575 and B576 in the OCR A specification.

OCR A Teacher Guide – Sikhism

ISBN 978-0-435-50127-3

This Teacher Guide covers Sikhism. It contains lesson plans, worksheets and Grade Studios to provide a complete teaching course for Sikhism. It covers Units B581 and B582 in the OCR A specification.

Assessment Objectives and Levels of Response

Assessment Objectives, AO1 and AO2

In the new specification, the questions in the examination are designed to test students against two Assessment Objectives: AO1 and AO2. In the specification 50 per cent of the marks will be awarded for AO1 questions and 50 per cent will be awarded for AO2 questions.

AO1 Questions require candidates to 'describe, explain and analyse, using knowledge and understanding'.

AO2 Questions require candidates to 'use evidence and reasoned argument to express and evaluate personal responses, informed insights, and differing viewpoints'.

Each question in the examination is composed of 5 parts, a–e. In more detail:

- Parts **a–c** are worth one, two and three marks respectively and test a candidate's knowledge (AO1 skills).
- Part **d** is worth six marks and tests a candidate's understanding (AO1 skills).
- Part **e** is worth twelve marks and tests a candidate's AO2 skills.

LEVELS OF RESPONSE FOR MARKING AO1 PART (D) QUESTIONS

LEVEL 1
(1–2 marks)

A **weak** attempt to answer the question.

Candidates will demonstrate little understanding of the question.

- A small amount of relevant information may be included.
- Answers may be in the form of a list with little or no description/explanation/analysis.
- There will be little or no use of specialist terms.
- Answers may be ambiguous or disorganised.
- Errors of grammar, punctuation and spelling may be intrusive.

LEVEL 2
(3–4 marks)

A **satisfactory** answer to the question.

Candidates will demonstrate some understanding of the question.

- Information will be relevant but may lack specific detail.
- There will be some description/explanation/analysis although this may not be fully developed.
- The information will be presented for the most part in a structured format.
- Some use of specialist terms, although these may not always be used appropriately.
- There may be errors in spelling, grammar and punctuation.

LEVEL 3
(5–6 marks)

A **good** answer to the question.

Candidates will demonstrate a clear understanding of the question.

- A fairly complete and full description/explanation/analysis.
- A comprehensive account of the range and depth of relevant material.
- The information will be presented in a structured format.
- There will be significant, appropriate and correct use of specialist terms.
- There will be few, if any, errors in spelling, grammar and punctuation.

LEVELS OF RESPONSE FOR MARKING AO2 PART (E) QUESTIONS

LEVEL 0

(0 marks)

No evidence submitted or response does not address the question.

LEVEL 1

(1–3 marks)

A **weak** attempt to answer the question.

Candidates will demonstrate little understanding of the question.

- Answers may be simplistic with little or no relevant information.
- Viewpoints may not be supported or appropriate.
- Answers may be ambiguous or disorganised.
- There will be little or no use of specialist terms.
- Errors of grammar, punctuation and spelling may be intrusive.

LEVEL 2

(4–6 marks)

A **limited** answer to the question.

Candidates will demonstrate some understanding of the question.

- Some information will be relevant, although may lack specific detail.
- Only one view might be offered and developed.
- Viewpoints might be stated and supported with limited argument/discussion.
- The information will show some organisation.
- Reference to the religion studied may be vague.
- Some use of specialist terms, although these may not always be used appropriately.
- There may be errors in spelling, grammar and punctuation.

LEVEL 3

(7–9 marks)

A **competent** answer to the question.

Candidates will demonstrate a sound understanding of the question.

- Selection of relevant material with appropriate development.
- Evidence of appropriate personal response.
- Justified arguments/different points of view supported by some discussion.
- The information will be presented in a structured format.
- Some appropriate reference to the religion studied.
- Specialist terms will be used appropriately and for the most part correctly.
- There may be occasional errors in spelling, grammar and punctuation.

LEVEL 4

(10–12 marks)

A **good** answer to the question.

Candidates will demonstrate a clear understanding of the question.

- Answers will reflect the significance of the issue(s) raised.
- Clear evidence of an appropriate personal response, fully supported.
- A range of points of view supported by justified arguments/discussion.
- The information will be presented in a clear and organised way.
- Clear reference to the religion studied.
- Specialist terms will be used appropriately and correctly.
- Few, if any, errors in spelling, grammar and punctuation.

Topic 1: Core beliefs

The Big Picture

In this Topic you will be addressing Jewish beliefs about:

- the nature of G-d
- Messiah and the Messianic Age
- the meaning and understanding of 'covenant'
- covenants with Abraham
- covenant with Moses
- the Law and the mitzvot
- beliefs about life after death.

You will also think about the ways in which these beliefs might affect the lifestyles and outlooks of Jews in the modern world.

What?

You will:

- develop your knowledge and understanding of key Jewish beliefs
- explain what these beliefs mean to Jews and think about how they might affect how Jews live
- make links between these beliefs and what you think/believe.

Why?

Because:

- these key Jewish beliefs underpin and are reflected in Jewish practices in all aspects of Jewish life and worship
- understanding Jewish beliefs can help you understand why Jews think and act in the way they do
- understanding these beliefs helps you to compare and contrast what others believe and to think about your own ideas/beliefs.

How?

By:

- recalling and selecting information about the key Jewish beliefs and explaining their importance to Jews today
- thinking about the relevance of Jewish beliefs in the context of the 21st century and the wider world
- reflecting on and evaluating your own views about these Jewish beliefs.

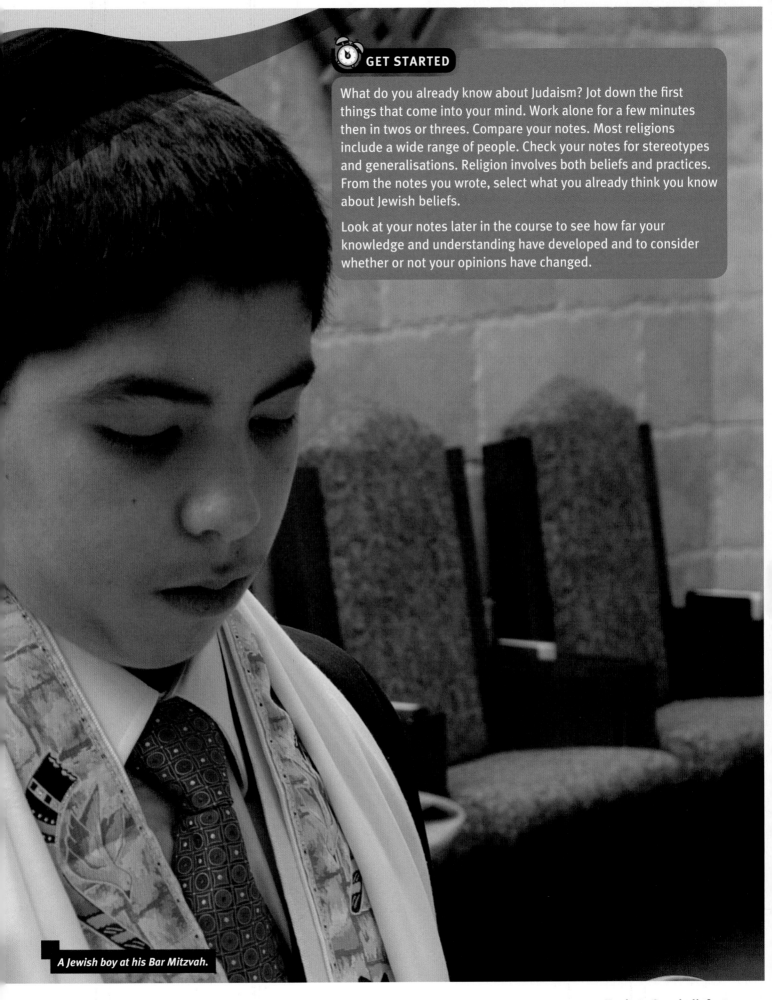

What do you already know about Judaism? Jot down the first things that come into your mind. Work alone for a few minutes then in twos or threes. Compare your notes. Most religions include a wide range of people. Check your notes for stereotypes and generalisations. Religion involves both beliefs and practices. From the notes you wrote, select what you already think you know about Jewish beliefs.

Look at your notes later in the course to see how far your knowledge and understanding have developed and to consider whether or not your opinions have changed.

A Jewish boy at his Bar Mitzvah.

Core beliefs

KEY INFORMATION

- Jewish belief is based on the idea that there is only one G-d.

- Jews are monotheists.

- Judaism is often described as 'the religion of the book' because it depends on its sacred writings as a source of authority.

- The Jewish Scriptures start with G-d creating the world and show that G-d sustains it and continues to be involved even in the events of human history.

- The Jewish Scriptures are called the **Tenakh**.

- The word Tenakh comes from the initial letters in Hebrew of **Torah** (Law), **Nevi'im** (Prophets) and **Ketuvim** (Writings).

- The Torah is the most important part of the Tenakh.

- Jews believe they have a special relationship with G-d called a covenant, which goes back to the time of Abraham.

- The Jewish Scriptures tell how Moses received the Law of the Covenant, including the Ten Commandments, from G-d on Mount Sinai to give to the Jewish nation.

- Jews follow a way of life called **Halakhah**, which in Hebrew means 'walking with G-d'. They live by the 613 **mitzvot** (commandments) found in the five books of Moses that make up the Torah.

- The centre of Jewish belief is contained in a prayer called the **Shema**. (Shema means 'Hear' in Hebrew.)

- One of the most significant events for all readers of the Jewish Scriptures is the Exodus from Egypt. Find out about it for homework.

- David and Solomon were two kings of Israel. Do any members of the class know anything about them?

- The Jewish Scriptures contain some books of prophecy. Prophets spoke out about the times in which they lived but also prophesied what would happen in the future. Do you believe that some people can foretell the future?

- Do you think G-d is in charge of history? Give reasons.

KNOWLEDGE AND UNDERSTANDING
What do Jews believe about G-d?

Did Jews still believe in their special relationship with G-d even in times of trouble and persecution?

What do I find interesting or puzzling about what Jews believe about G-d?

What do I believe about G-d and why do I believe it?

ANALYSIS AND EVALUATION
How can G-d be all powerful when such awful things happen in the world?

Can books that were written so long ago still be important to Jews today?

KEY WORDS

belief Something held to be true.

covenant G-d's promise to help the people of Israel.

faith Trust, confidence in and commitment to something or someone.

Halakhah Hebrew for 'walking with G-d'; putting Jewish beliefs into practice, living a Jewish life.

holy Sacred; morally and spiritually perfect; separate from contamination and to be shown reverence.

Judaism The religion of the Jews.

Messiah A leader or deliverer sent by G-d to bring in a Messianic Age of peace.

Mitzvah Commandment. The Torah contains 613 mitzvot.

monotheist A person who believes in one G-d.

omnipotent G-d is all powerful.

omnipresent G-d is everywhere and at all times.

religion System of belief and practice – way of life built on belief in the divine (G-d).

Shema A Jewish prayer affirming belief in one G-d. It is found in the Torah.

Tenakh The collected 35 books of the Jewish Bible, comprising three sections: Torah, Nevi'im and Ketuvim (Te;Na;Kh).

Torah Law or teaching. The five books of Moses in the Scriptures.

transcendent G-d is beyond the physical/natural world.

FOR INTEREST With 12 million followers, Judaism is actually one of the smallest of the world faiths yet it seems to have enormous influence in the world.

The nature of G-d (1)

The next two pages will help you to:

- explore the question 'Is G-d the creator?'
- evaluate if there is a G-d and ask 'What is G-d like?'

Many people see the power of G-d in the natural world.

G-d as Creator

> ### Genesis 1:3–5
>
> *G-d said, there be light; and there was light. G-d saw that the light was good, and G-d separated the light from the darkness. G-d called the light Day, and the darkness He called Night. And there was evening and there was morning, a first day.*

This is how the Jewish Scriptures begin. From the very first sentence it is assumed that G-d exists. In our modern world there are some people who do not believe in G-d or gods; but for most religious people, **belief** in a creator is the starting point of their **faith**. All people wonder about questions such as, 'How did the world begin?', 'Why are we here?' and 'What is life all about?'

Science provides some answers but these ultimate questions also provoke religious responses. Scientific and mathematical theories are tested and some are proved eventually to be facts. Beliefs are a matter of faith. Believers accept them as true because something in their own experience has convinced them.

ACTIVITIES

Write down seven adjectives that might describe G-d. Compare with a friend and make your two lists into one list of seven words. Try to put your words in order of importance. Then join another pair to make the best list of seven words that you can. See what the rest of the class selected.

G-d as King of the Universe

Jews not only believe that G-d created the universe but also that he sustains it. He continues to rule and control everything. G-d is almighty. He is **omnipotent**, having the power to do anything. He is omniscient, knowing everything. He is **omnipresent**; G-d is everywhere. No one can hide from G-d.

These descriptions of the nature or characteristics of G-d make him seem mysterious and beyond human understanding. This is the transcendence of G-d. It causes humans to feel fear, awe, wonder and respect as they worship G-d, the King of the Universe.

Jews believe not only in the transcendence of G-d but also in the immanence of G-d. This means he is close to and cares for even the smallest part of his creation.

The relationship between G-d and humanity

The relationship between G-d and humanity is found right at the beginning of the Scriptures in the first account of Creation in Genesis. G-d decided to create humans in his own image and to give them authority over the earth and all life on it. He also gave the first instruction to humans that they were to populate the earth:

> **Genesis 1:26–28, 31**
>
> *And G-d said, 'Let us make man in our image, after our likeness. They shall rule the fish of the sea, the birds of the sky, the cattle, the whole earth, and all the creeping things that creep on earth.' And G-d created man in His image, in the image of G-d He created him; male and female He created them. G-d blessed them and G-d said to them, 'Be fertile and increase, fill the earth and master it; and rule the fish of the sea, the birds of the sky, and all the living things that creep on earth.'... And it was so. And G-d saw all that He had made, and found it very good. And there was evening and there was morning, the sixth day.*

Humans were made in G-d's image. What do you think that means? Ruling the earth on behalf of G-d is often called stewardship. For people of all religious persuasions, belief in G-d as Creator has implications concerning the treatment of the world.

AO1 skills ACTIVITIES

What leads people to believe? Ask two or three people in your class what they think.

AO2 skills ACTIVITIES

For a whole weekend try to focus more than usual on creation; notice everything around you, every natural feature including the stars at night. Study something that is large, such as the sky or a landscape, and something that is small, such as an insect or a flower. Try to write a short poem to express your thoughts.

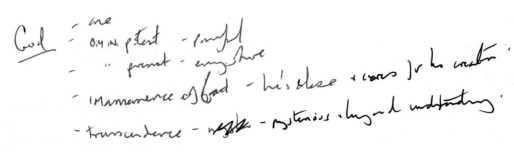

The nature of G-d (2)

The next two pages will help you to:

- analyse the particular characteristics of G-d according to the Jews
- examine the importance for Jews of belief in G-d.

St Catherine's monastery at the foot of Mount Sinai, Egypt.

The characteristics of G-d

Jews believe that G-d is the creator of the universe and everything in it, that G-d has a purpose for the world and that G-d knows everything and can do anything. It is therefore important for Jews to know what the character of G-d is like.

It is important because Jews believe that:

- G-d is beyond time and space
- G-d is everywhere all the time
- G-d is interested in how people behave
- G-d judges each individual
- G-d is omnibenevolent – all-good and all-loving.

It is therefore important for Jews to live the way G-d wants them to live. How do people who believe in G-d find out what G-d wants? In particular, how do Jews find out? Are there any 'best' ways?

Jews will try to find out how G-d wants them to behave from the Jewish Scriptures, the Tenakh and, in particular, the Torah.

Jews believe that:
- G-d chose to reveal himself to human beings
- G-d made laws based on his own characteristics such as justice and mercy
- G-d inspired prophets to speak his words.

ACTIVITIES

In pairs, look up two references from Psalm 23; Hosea 11:1–4; Jeremiah 31:32; 1 Kings 19:11–12. How is G-d described? Make notes and compare your notes with other pairs.

Though Jews do not make images of G-d, the writers of the Jewish Scriptures often describe G-d in picture language such as similies and metaphors, e.g. G-d caring like a shepherd, ruling like a king or opening the windows of heaven to pour out a blessing. This can help us to understand what Jews believe the character of G-d is like.

The Jewish Scriptures do not try to define G-d. They describe the nature of G-d by what G-d has done, does and will do. It is important to remember that, to the Jews, G-d is the Lord of History – past, present and future. Jews believe that G-d has shown love to his people throughout history. The Hebrew word for this love is 'hesed'.

The Chosen People – G-d's special role for the Jews

> **Deuteronomy 14:2**
>
> *For you are a people consecrated to the LORD your G-d: the LORD your G-d chose you from among all other peoples on earth to be His treasured people.*

Jews believe that they have a special relationship with G-d. This does not mean that Jews think they are better than other people. Jews are called 'the Chosen People' in the Torah because G-d said that they had a special responsibility to the rest of humanity to set an example of how G-d wanted people to live according to his will.

The central statement of Jewish belief in G-d is found in the prayer called the Shema, which Jews say several times a day. The Shema contains instructions about how Jews should live and how they should bring up their children.

The Shema consists of three passages from the Torah: Deuteronomy 6:4–9, 11:13–21, Numbers 15:37–41.

> **Deuteronomy 11:18–21**
>
> *Therefore impress these My words upon your very heart: bind them as a sign on your hand and let them serve as a symbol on your forehead, and teach them to your children – reciting them when you stay at home and when you are away, when you lie down and when you get up; and inscribe them on the doorposts of your house and on your gates – to the end that you and your children may endure, in the land that the LORD swore to your fathers to assign to them, as long as there is a heaven over the earth.*

> **Numbers 15:37–41**
>
> *The LORD said to Moses as follows: Speak to the Israelite people and instruct them to make for themselves fringes on the corners of their garments throughout the ages; let them attach a cord of blue to the fringe at each corner. That shall be your fringe; look at it and recall all the commandments of the LORD and observe them, so that you do not follow your heart and eyes in your lustful urge. Thus you shall be reminded to observe all My commandments and to be holy to your G-d. I the LORD am your G-d, who brought you out of the land of Egypt to be your G-d: I, the LORD your G-d.*

ACTIVITIES

In pairs discuss the key ideas in these two passages from the Shema. How far do you agree that this statement of belief in one G-d is at the centre of Jewish life? To what extent do you think these passages read like a contract?

Messiah and the Messianic Age

The next two pages will help you to:

- explore the Jewish concept of the perfect world in a Messianic Age
- analyse the characteristics of a Messiah.

The perfect world

Jews believe that:

- G-d is the Creator, the Lord of the Beginning of all things and the Sustainer of the Universe
- G-d is the Lord of History and has a plan for history (past, present and future)
- G-d is the Lord of the End of all things.

The Messianic Age

The Messianic Age is a theological term for a future time of peace on earth without crime, war and poverty. Many **religions** believe in such an age. Many non-religious people hope for it too.

AO1 skills ACTIVITIES

Look up the word 'utopia'. What does it mean?

> **Micah 4:1–3**
>
> *In the days to come,*
> *The Mount of the LORD's House shall stand*
> *Firm above the mountains;*
> *And it shall tower above the hills.*
> *The peoples shall gaze on it with joy,*
> *And the many nations shall go and shall say:*
> *'Come,*
> *Let us go up to the Mount of the LORD,*
> *To the House of the G-d of Jacob;*
> *That He may instruct us in His ways,*
> *And that we may walk in His paths.'*
> *For instruction shall come forth from Zion,*
> *The word of the LORD from Jerusalem.*
> *Thus He will judge among the many peoples,*
> *And arbitrate for the multitude of nations,*
> *However distant;*
> *And they shall beat their swords into ploughshares*
> *And their spears into pruning hooks.*
> *Nation shall not take up*
> *Sword against nation;*
> *They shall never again know war.*

REMEMBER THIS

Tikkun olam: literally 'repair of the world'. Some Jews, besides believing in a Messiah or Messiahs, also believe that the time of universal peace will be the result of tikkun olam through human efforts towards the social justice that the Torah and the prophets say G-d desires.

In **Judaism**, this time of peace on earth will be under the rule of a Messiah or 'Anointed One', who will be sent by G-d. Jews believe that in this Messianic Age G-d's values and teachings found in the Torah will be followed by all people of the world and that there will be justice and harmony throughout the world with no more warfare or suffering.

Read the description of the Jewish idea of the perfect world after the coming of the Messiah in Micah 4:1–3.

Characteristics of the Messiah

'Messiah' means 'Anointed One' and people such as kings, priests and prophets were anointed in the Jewish Scriptures. The ancient practice of anointing with holy oil, signified being chosen for a task (particularly divinely chosen).

Even Cyrus, a non-Jewish king, was called 'Hashem's Anointed One' because he had performed a task that accorded with the will of G-d (Isaiah 45:1). There are many teachings about the Messiah in the writings of the prophets in the Jewish Scriptures, particularly in the books of Micah, Isaiah and Malachi.

The characteristics of the Messiah can be found in Isaiah 9:5–6. This passage says that the Messiah will be born and have the authority of G-d on his shoulders. He will be a peaceful ruler and introduce a time of peace that will last forever. He will sit on the traditional throne of King David in Jerusalem and will rule justly over the world.

According to some scholars, oracles such as these were given at the birth or accession to the throne of each king of the Davidic line of succession. Remember that David was not only seen as a king but also as a shepherd.

> **1 Samuel 10:1**
> *Samuel took a flask of oil and poured some on Saul's head and kissed him, and said, 'The Lord herewith anoints you ruler over His own people.'*

The idea of the Messiah

When the Jews went into exile in Babylon in 587 BCE and had lost their land, their city – Jerusalem, their Temple and their king, they learnt to trust in G-d that these things would be restored and G-d's plan for his people and the world would be fulfilled in G-d's appointed time.

During the period of Roman rule in the first centuries CE the idea of a Messiah became very important in Jewish thought and teaching. There were several revolts in Palestine during the reign of Herod the Great and his successors, and a number of prophets gained large followings and were claimed as the Messiah who was to come. Jesus of Nazareth was seen as one of these and his followers called him the Christ (Greek for 'Anointed One').

The Romans destroyed the Jerusalem Temple in 70 CE. Jewish revolts continued and in 132–35 CE a revolt was led by Simon bar Kochba who people claimed was the Messiah. This revolt was put down by Julius Severus.

Claims of a new Messiah have continued to the present day but, for most Jews, the Messiah is someone they are still waiting for and who will establish the golden Messianic Age. It has been said that in every generation a person is born with the potential to be the Messiah. It has also been said that if all the Jews kept the Sabbath properly for two weeks, the Messiah would come. Some Jews speak of two Messiahs: Messiah son of David and a suffering Messiah descended from Joseph, son of Jacob/Israel.

ACTIVITIES

The Jews believe they have a special relationship with G-d that is based on the idea of covenant and is significant in bringing about G-d's purposes for the world.

'Jews have waited too long for a Messiah and should give up hope of him arriving.' Do you agree with this statement? How might a Jew respond?

The meaning and understanding of 'covenant'

The next two pages will help you to:

- examine the concept of covenant
- explore the meaning, importance and significance of the covenants in the Jewish Scriptures.

For centuries people have searched for the remains of Noah's Ark on Mount Ararat in Turkey. Recently Mount Sabalan in Iran has been suggested as the final resting place of the Ark.

The concept of covenant

Historians and archaeologists have evidence that, in ancient times, there were treaties resembling the covenants of the Jewish Scriptures. For example, there were treaties between the Great King of the Hittites and his vassal subjects.

'Covenant' is defined as a promise, testament or agreement. Sometimes the word 'contract' is used. The concept of the covenant between G-d and the Jewish people does have elements of a contract but it also involves feelings such as trust, loyalty and love ('hesed'). Sometimes there are signs, sacrifices and other features that are of significance in covenants and worth comparing, but the key to all the covenants in the Jewish Scriptures is the fact that G-d takes the initiative and starts the encounter.

The beliefs of the Jewish faith are not rooted in philosophy. Judaism is based on history and experience. The story of the Jewish nation begins when Abraham obeyed G-d's command and went to a new country.

Generations later the deliverance from Egypt and the journey back to the Promised Land led to the establishing of the Covenant Law, the Torah. When the Jewish Scriptures were written down they described, in a variety of types of literature, the different ways in which G-d had been made known through the experience of Israel.

ACTIVITIES

Have you ever made a pact with somebody? Have you seen a film where two tribes make a treaty? What do people do in such situations? Do they make a symbolic action, sign something or drink a toast to the agreement? What happens when one of them breaks the deal?

The covenant G-d made with Adam

The Jewish Scriptures do not begin with Abraham; they begin with Creation. Whether the account of Adam and Eve in the Garden of Eden is taken literally or not, it expresses the belief that the covenant story starts with the creation of humankind and G-d's plan for the whole of humanity. The covenant with Adam can be found in Genesis 1–3. G-d gave instructions as to what humanity had power over, what people were to do, what they were not to do, and a command to begin the work.

The covenant G-d made with Noah

The covenant with Noah is found in Genesis 9. Here, after destroying almost all life in the flood, G-d promises that:

> **Genesis 9:11b**
> *Never again shall all flesh be cut off by the waters of a flood, and never again shall there be a flood to destroy the earth.*

G-d then gave a sign of the covenant.

G-d further said:

> **Genesis 9:12–13**
> *This is the sign that I set for the covenant between Me and you, and every living creature with you, for all ages to come. I have set My bow in the clouds, and it shall serve as a sign of the covenant between Me and the earth.*

At the time of making the covenant with Noah, G-d gave commands that had to be obeyed. These are known as the Noachide Code. Judaism teaches that any religion that keeps all the laws of the Noachide Code is an acceptable way for non-Jews to serve G-d.

- Do not worship images or idols.
- Do not commit blasphemy or curse G-d.
- Do not commit murder.
- Do not steal.
- Do not commit adultery.
- Do not eat a limb of a live animal (this is usually taken to mean that all cruelty to animals is prohibited).
- Set up a legal system and promote justice.

A list of these seven mitzvot (commandments) is found in the **Talmud**.

RESEARCH NOTE

Study the covenant G-d made with Noah and his sons after the Flood. What sign does G-d give as part of the agreement?

ACTIVITIES

'If people make promises to G-d then they should be punished if they break them.' What do you think? How might a Jew respond to this?

> **Sanhedrin 56a**
> *The Rabbis taught: seven precepts were the sons of Noah commanded: social laws; to refrain from blasphemy; idolatry; adultery; bloodshed; robbery; and eating flesh cut from a living animal.*

Covenants with Abraham

The next two pages will help you to:

- explore the three covenants G-d made with Abraham
- explore the significance to Jews of the three covenants
- examine the question 'What is different about being children of Abraham?'

Abraham prepares to sacrifice Isaac (Genesis 22:1–19).

AO1 skills ACTIVITIES

For the Jews the covenant starts with Abraham. What do you already know about Abraham?

When did Abraham live and where was he born? Find out where Abraham's tomb is.

Abraham was a monotheist: he believed in one G-d. To Abraham this was not simply an idea in his head. He had so much faith in G-d that he left his home with his family and set out on a long journey to a new land, because he believed G-d wanted him to do so. Abraham had to avoid the desert areas so he went north between two great rivers: the Tigris and the Euphrates. The Scriptures say that his father, Terah, died when they got to Haran. While Abraham and his family were living in Haran, Abraham received the first of the three covenants from G-d. This covenant applied to his family and all his descendants, the Israelites. From Haran, they then turned south and went down the coast to the Promised Land.

Genesis 12:1–3

The LORD said to Abram, 'Go forth from your native land and from your father's house to the land that I will show you.
I will make of you a great nation,
And I will bless you;
I will make your name great,
And you shall be a blessing.
I will bless those who bless you
And curse him that curses you;
And all the families of the earth
Shall bless themselves by you.'

The first covenant

In the first covenant G-d tells Abraham that he will live with his family in the Promised Land.

The second covenant

In the second covenant G-d promises children to Abraham and repeats the promise of land. Abraham sacrifices some of his livestock for G-d. This practice of 'cutting' animals still happens in some parts of the world today.

> ### Genesis 15:5–14
>
> *He took him outside and said, 'Look toward heaven and count the stars, if you are able to count them.' And He added, 'So shall your offspring be.' And because he put his trust in the LORD, He reckoned it to his merit.*
>
> *Then He said to him, 'I am the LORD who brought you out from Ur of the Chaldeans to assign this land to you as a possession.' And he said, 'O Lord G-D, how shall I know that I am to possess it?' He answered, 'Bring Me a three-year-old heifer, a three-year-old she-goat, a three-year-old ram, a turtledove, and a young bird.' He brought Him all these and cut them in two, placing each half opposite the other; but he did not cut up the bird. Birds of prey came down upon the carcasses, and Abram drove them away. As the sun was about to set, a deep sleep fell upon Abram, and a great dark dread descended upon him. And He said to Abram, 'Know well that your offspring shall be strangers in a land not theirs, and they shall be enslaved and oppressed four hundred years; but I will execute judgment on the nation they shall serve, and in the end they shall go free with great wealth.'*

After the sacrifice G-d makes a promise of land to Abraham's descendants:

> ### Genesis 15:18b
>
> *To your offspring I assign this land, from the river of Egypt to the great river, the river Euphrates.*

The third covenant

In the third covenant G-d makes promises to Abraham but requires that all male Jews are to be circumcised as part of the covenant.

The three covenants between G-d and Abraham show the distinctiveness that G-d placed on the Jews. All Jews are 'children of Abraham' and are bound by these covenants. This places particular responsibilities on Jews.

ACTIVITIES

Jews, Christians and Muslims all see themselves as 'children of Abraham' in that they all believe in the same G-d as Abraham believed in, and put their trust in G-d. Do you think that this common belief could be used to solve any of the conflicts in the world today? Give reasons. Consider other points of view.

Covenant with Moses

The next two pages will help you to:

- examine the importance of Moses and the Exodus to the Jews
- consider the impact of the Ten Commandments up to the present day.

Moses received the Ten Commandments from G-d on Mount Sinai.

The covenant with Abraham was the start of the story of the Jews but the covenant that Moses mediated between G-d and the Jewish people was the start of the Jewish nation. Whenever the Jews want to remind themselves of the character of G-d they turn to the story of the Exodus from Egypt. The Jews were helpless and weak but G-d freely showed his grace and mercy.

This event took place between 1350 and 1200 BCE. Many Jewish people were living in Egypt. The Pharaoh of Egypt had made the Jews become slaves. Moses, who was a Jew but had been brought up at the Egyptian court, felt called by G-d to rescue the Jews. He gave Pharaoh this message from G-d: 'Let my people go!' Pharaoh refused and ten plagues fell on Egypt.

AO1 skills **ACTIVITIES**

How many of the Ten Commandments do you know? Where was Moses when he was given the Ten Commandments? What was the Ark of the Covenant?

Eventually Pharaoh let the slaves go and they began their long trek through the wilderness to the Promised Land. They had to cross the Red Sea and, by then, Pharaoh had changed his mind and the Egyptian army was pursuing them. The story is in the book of Exodus. It has inspired people besides Jews when they have needed freedom from oppression and captivity.

The covenant with Moses, sometimes called the Sinai Covenant, was made during the time the Jews were wandering through the desert near Mount Sinai. The most important part of this covenant is the Ten Commandments. Together with the Shema, the Ten Commandments form the basis of Jewish belief.

RESEARCH NOTE

There was much more, however, that G-d told Moses on Sinai. Find out about the Oral Torah.

Exodus 20:2–14

I the LORD am your G-d who brought you out of the land of Egypt, the house of bondage: You shall have no other Gods besides Me.

You shall not make for yourself a sculptured image, or any likeness of what is in the heavens above, or on the earth below, or in the waters under the earth. You shall not bow down to them or serve them. For I the LORD your G-d am an impassioned G-d, visiting the guilt of the parents upon the children, upon the third and upon the fourth generations of those who reject Me, but showing kindness to the thousandth generation of those who love Me and keep My commandments.

You shall not swear falsely by the name of the LORD your G-d; for the LORD will not clear one who swears falsely by His name.

Remember the sabbath day and keep it holy. Six days you shall labour and do all your work, but the seventh day is a sabbath of the LORD your G-d: you shall not do any work – you, your son or daughter, your male or female slave, or your cattle, or the stranger who is within your settlements. For in six days the LORD made heaven and earth and sea, and all that is in them, and He rested on the seventh day; therefore the LORD blessed the sabbath day and hallowed it.

Honour your father and your mother, that you may long endure on the land that the LORD your G-d is assigning to you.

You shall not murder.

You shall not commit adultery.

You shall not steal.

You shall not bear false witness against your neighbour.

You shall not covet your neighbour's house: you shall not covet your neighbour's wife, or his male or female slave, or his ox or his ass, or anything that is your neighbour's.

G-d had delivered the Jews from Egypt. In return they had to keep his commands. The Jews were supposed to be a kingdom of priests; they were supposed to live as an example of how G-d wanted all people to live.

When Moses gave the covenant to the Jewish nation they responded, 'We hear and obey!'

The Ten Commandments are central to Jewish life and belief. Although Judaism teaches that there are 613 mitzvot (commandments) that have to be obeyed, the Ten Commandments remain central for the life of a Jew.

They show how Jews should worship G-d and respond to him as well as how they should treat others.

AO2 skills **ACTIVITIES**

Compare the Ten Commandments with the Noachide Code.

The Law and the mitzvot

A tallit or prayer shawl worn by Jewish men for prayer.

The concept of Law

The Torah that contains the five books of Moses – Genesis, Exodus, Leviticus, Numbers and Deuteronomy – is called the 'Law' or 'teaching'. The word 'Torah' means 'direction' or 'instruction' but is usually translated as 'Law'. The Law of the Torah, both written and oral, is central to Jewish faith and belief. For Jews, the Torah contains the divinely revealed word of G-d, given directly by G-d to Moses on Mount Sinai. It is therefore absolute truth and must be obeyed. The Ten Commandments (see Topic 1.6) are central to rules about life, behaviour and worship.

However, rabbis later worked through the text of the Torah and ruled that there were actually 613 commandments that Jews must obey. These are known as the 613 mitzvot. They include the Ten Commandments of the Sinai Covenant.

The mitzvot

A mitzvah is a commandment or religious duty. There are several different groupings of mitzvot:

- the 613 mitzvot, which are divided into 248 Mitzvot aseh (positive commandments that say what must be followed) and 365 Mitzvot lo ta'aseh (negative commandments that say what is forbidden)
- Mitzvot de-oraita: biblical mitzvot
- Mitzvot de-rabbanan: rabbinical mitzvot
- Mitzvot kallot: less important commandments
- Mitzvot hamurot: more important commandments.

Despite these distinctions, the rabbis ruled that all the mitzvot must be observed. However, some can only be observed in Israel and some rely on the Temple being in Jerusalem. Therefore, although Jews in Israel are bound by more of the mitzvot than those in the **diaspora**, there are still some mitzvot that Jews have not been able to observe fully since the destruction of the Jerusalem Temple in 70 CE and cannot observe unless the Temple is rebuilt.

Males take on all the mitzvot when they are one day past their 13th birthday. Girls have to take on this responsibility when they are a day past their 12th birthday. This is the reason that coming of age ceremonies such as Bar Mitzvah (see page 112–13) take place at this time. However, although women have to observe all the Mitzvot lo ta'aseh, they do not have to carry out all the Mizvot aseh associated with festivals. Women are exempt from time-based mitzvot such as those concerning the shofar, the sukkah, the lulav, the tzizit and tefillin.

The different rules for men and women are often explained on the basis that women are naturally more spiritual and are therefore closer to G-d so do not need so many rules to be able to live as G-d wants. Also, some of the time-based mitzvot could interfere with their duties and obligations to their families.

There are several lists of the 613 mitzvot, one of the best know being the Sefer Hamitzvot (Book of Commandments) by Maimonides (see page 145). The opposite of a mitzvah is an averah – a sin.

Judaism teaches that people can only really be happy and fulfilled if they live according to the 613 mitzvot. There is no promise of immediate reward on earth for keeping the mitzvot – they are simply part of a Jew's duty to G-d. However, Judaism teaches that people can only be truly happy and content when they do keep them.

With so many rules and instructions, observing the mitzvot is inevitably a very important part of Jewish daily life, and Jews try to observe these today as they did in the past.

> **Makkoth 3:16**
> *G-d desired to make Israel worthy, therefore He enlarged the Law and multiplied its mitzvot.*

ACTIVITIES

'No one can be expected to keep so many rules. Jews should just stick to the Ten Commandments.' Do you agree with this statement? How do you think a Jew would respond?

Beliefs about life after death

The next two pages will help you to:

- understand Jewish beliefs about life after death
- examine the importance of these beliefs for Jews.

Gan Eden.

AO1 skills **ACTIVITIES**

Explain to a partner what you think happens after people die and give reasons for your ideas.

Gehenna.

Sheol.

Life after death

Unlike some religions, Judaism does not have any specific teaching about the relationship between the body and the soul, and this is not considered to be important. Jews believe that G-d breathed the soul into Adam's body, as stated in Genesis 2:7.

In explaining this, the rabbis said that the soul leaves the body during sleep and then draws refreshment from heaven. It leaves the body at death but body and soul are eventually reunited at the end of time. The rabbis taught that the body and soul cannot survive without each other.

On **Shabbat** (the Sabbath ordered in the fourth of the Ten Commandments), tradition says that G-d gives each body an extra soul, but this is taken back at **Havdalah** (the ceremony marking the conclusion of Shabbat).

At the time when most of the Jewish Scriptures were written, people believed that after death everyone went to **Sheol**. This is described as a dark place where people went after death and stayed for eternity. This belief arises from the idea that Adam and Eve would have lived forever in the Garden of Eden, but when they disobeyed G-d they became mortal. Since then, everyone has grown old and eventually died.

These beliefs were later clarified and the first mention of a resurrection of the dead comes in the book of Daniel.

> **Genesis 2:7**
>
> *The Lord G-d formed man from the dust of the earth. He blew into his nostrils the breath of life, and man became a living being.*

> **Daniel 12:2–3**
>
> *Many of those that sleep in the dust of the earth will awake, some to eternal life, others to reproaches, to everlasting abhorrence. And the knowledgeable will be radiant like the bright expanse of sky, and those who lead the many to righteousness will be like the stars forever and ever.*

Heaven and hell

Beliefs about heaven and hell come much later in Jewish thought. By the 2nd century BCE some Jews had come to believe that Sheol was a place where the dead would wait until the Day of Judgement.

Some people said that the righteous would enter **Gan Eden** (Paradise) while the wicked would go to **Gehenna** (Gehinnom) after the last judgement. Some rabbis, however, said that the dead would go to these places immediately after death.

Gehenna is not the same as Sheol. Sheol was seen as a place of waiting, whereas Gehenna was hell. When someone is judged by G-d, the body and soul will be reunited; the accuser will be the soul, and the body cannot blame the soul for its actions. Jews believe that this judgement will take place after the coming of the Messiah.

Towards the end of the period when the Jewish Scriptures were written, some of them explained that there might be an eternal life with G-d after death. They also believed that eventually G-d would judge people and that those who had not lived according to G-d's will would go to hell.

A development of the ideas of the afterlife is found in the second book of Maccabees where a mother and her seven sons are killed for refusing to deny G-d:

> **2 Maccabees 7:9**
> …the King of the universe will raise us up to an everlasting renewal of life…

So, although Jews believe that they may be punished or rewarded after death for the way in which they have lived their lives, there is no clear teaching about heaven in the Jewish Scriptures.

For Jews the importance of life is the way in which it is lived on earth. Whatever may happen after death is in G-d's hands and should be left to G-d to arrange. Therefore, Judaism is a religion that puts great stress and importance on the way people live their lives, not on how this may affect their soul. This emphasis is found in a number of Jewish practices. For example, when Jews make a toast over a drink they say 'L'Chaim' – 'to life', and traditional Jewish birthday cards say 'May you live to be 120.' These examples show that Judaism is concerned with life, rather than with what might happen afterwards.

To live a good life, Jews must follow the Ten Commandments and the 613 mitzvot, they must live a halakhic life (walking with G-d) and treat others well. This is the most that anyone can do – it is left to G-d to decide what, if anything, will happen next.

AO2 skills ACTIVITIES

'If Jews believe in G-d then they must believe in life after death.' Do you agree with this statement? How might a Jew respond to this?

Welcome to the Grade Studio

In this Grade Studio we will look at the longer AO1 responses required for part (d) of the question, which is worth 6 marks. Part (d) of each question will be marked according to levels. For AO1, there are three levels. A good response to part (d) will be well organised, contain relevant knowledge and will have a full, well-developed explanation. If required, you should analyse the Topic, which means you might make a comparison between two aspects of the Topic.

Graded examples for this topic

AO1

AO1 questions test what you know and how well you can explain and analyse things. Let's look at an AO1 question to see what examiners expect you to do.

Question

Explain why the mitzvot are important for Jewish life.   **[6 marks]**

Student's answer

> The mitzvot are commandments.

Examiner's comment

This is a start to responding to the question, but the answer is very weak. There is no real explanation. This response is only Level 1.

Student's improved answer

> The mitzvot are commandments. There are 613 mitzvot, which include the Ten Commandments. Adult Jews must keep all 613 of them although women do not have to keep all the mitzvot that relate to festivals. They are divided into different groups, such as more and less important, positive and negative, and ones that are from the Scriptures and ones that are from the rabbis. In order to live a halakhic life it is essential for Jews to keep all the mitzvot.

Examiner's comment

This is an excellent answer. The candidate could have limited their answer to just some examples and perhaps explained them in more depth, but this is another way of answering the question where all different types of mitzvot are considered.

AO2

AO2 questions are about examining points of view and expressing your own views, using evidence and argument to support them. AO2 questions are worth 12 marks.

Examiners will use levels of response to judge the quality of your work and the best responses will have plenty of evidence to support different points of view. For AO2 there are four levels of response and for the top level the response will have a personal view supported by evidence and argument.

Question

'Only the Covenant of Circumcision is really important – the others don't matter.' Discuss this statement. You should include different, supported points of view and a personal viewpoint. You must refer to Judaism in your answer.

[12 marks]

Student's answer	Examiner's comment
The Covenant of Circumcision was made with Abraham and every male Jew has to be circumcised. I agree that this is the most important one because it is about people and being a Jew.	This is a better response. The answer gives an explanation of a possible Jewish view. However, it only gives one view and a personal opinion and so can only reach Level 2.

Student's improved answer	Examiner's comment
The Covenant of Circumcision was made with Abraham and every male Jew has to be circumcised. This is obviously very important but the other covenants are also important. The Sinai Covenant is important because this was when G-d gave the Ten Commandments to Moses. The covenants that give the Promised Land to Abraham and his descendants are also important, as is the agreement that the Jews will always worship G-d and obey his commandments. I agree that the Covenant of Circumcision is the most important one because it is about people and being a Jew, and without following it a male cannot be a Jew.	This is a very good answer. It gives clear explanations of two possible Jewish views, as well as personal opinions. This reaches Level 4.

These specimen answers provide an outline of how you could construct your response. Space does not allow us to give a full response. The examiner will be looking for more detail in your actual exam responses.

Remember and Reflect

AO1 Describe, explain and analyse, using knowledge and understanding

Find the answer on:

1 Explain, in one sentence, what each of the following key words means:
  a covenant
  b Messiah
  c Sheol

PAGE 5, 11, 21

2 What are the mitzvot?

PAGE 19

3 Explain what is meant by monotheism.

PAGE 5

4 Explain why the Torah is important to Jews.

PAGE 18

5 Explain what each of these words means:
  a Gan Eden
  b Halakhah

PAGE 5, 21

6 Explain, giving examples, the important teachings of the Shema.

PAGE 9

7 Explain, in one sentence, what each of the following words means:
  a omnipotent
  b omnipresent

PAGE 5, 7

8 Outline three of the covenants.

PAGE 12–17

9 Explain why circumcision is important.

PAGE 23

10 Explain beliefs about Sheol, Gan Eden and Gehenna.

PAGE 20, 21

11 Explain the importance of what is said when Jews make a toast.

PAGE 21

12 Explain how Adam received his soul.

PAGE 20

13 What was the first instruction given by G-d to humanity?

PAGE 7

14 Give an example of a time-based mitzvah.

PAGE 19

15 When will judgement take place?

PAGE 21

16 When do people have two souls?

PAGE 20

17 Explain the difference between Mizvot kallot and Mitzvot hamurot.

PAGE 19

18 How is the word 'Tenakh' made up?

PAGE 4, 5

AO2 Use evidence and reasoned argument to express and evaluate personal responses, informed insights, and differing viewpoints

1 Answer the following, giving as much detail as possible. You should give at least three reasons to support your response, and also show that you have taken into account opposite opinions.

   a *Jews find following all the mitzvot difficult. Do you think ancient religious laws are relevant in today's world?*

   b *Do you believe the Laws in the Torah came from G-d? Why or why not? Compare your response with that of a Jew and an atheist.*

2 'Belief in a Messiah is simply out of date.' How would a Jew answer this? Refer to Jewish teaching and practice.

3 'It really doesn't matter which day of the week people rest.'

   'Jewish beliefs about life after death don't offer any hope.'

   'The Noachide Code is enough, people don't need another 606 laws.'

   What do you think about these statements? Give reasons for your answers, showing that you have thought about it from more than one point of view.

Topic 2: Special days and pilgrimage

The Big Picture

In this Topic you will be exploring the nature of Jewish special days and pilgrimage. You will understand the importance of:

- Shabbat
- Rosh Hashanah
- Yom Kippur
- the pilgrim festivals:
  - Pesach
  - Shavuot
  - Sukkot.

You will also consider the significance of these special days for Jews as individuals and communities, as well as the role pilgrimage has played in the spiritual life of Judaism.

What?

You will:
- understand how and why the special days came into being
- understand the pilgrim festivals and the importance of pilgrimage to Judaism.

Why?

Because:
- it is important to understand the place of special days in Judaism and their influence on the beliefs and practices of Jews
- it is important to understand why the nature of pilgrimage in Judaism has changed.

How?

By:
- examining the origins and nature of the special days and pilgrim festivals
- understanding the importance of the special days and pilgrimage
- evaluating your own views about the role and importance of pilgrimage and celebrations.

In the Ten Commandments Jews are told to keep Shabbat.

> **Exodus 20:8–11**
>
> *Remember the Sabbath day to sanctify it. Six days shall you work and accomplish all your work; but the seventh day is Sabbath to Hashem, your G-d; You shall not do any work – you, your son, your daughter, your slave, your maidservant, your animal, and your convert within your gates – for in six days Hashem made the heavens and the earth, the sea and all that is in them, and He rested on the seventh day. Therefore, Hashem blessed the Sabbath day and sanctified it.*

Importance of Shabbat for Jews

Shabbat is very important because it gives a Jewish family a weekly chance to spend a day together without any interruptions from work. Instead they can worship together at home and at the **synagogue**.

Shabbat begins 18 minutes before sunset on Friday. The most senior woman in the household lights two candles, which welcome the festival into the home. The candles are lit before sunset to make sure that no work is done on Shabbat as candle-lighting would count as work. As sunset is at different times throughout the year many Jews begin early in the summer rather than waiting late to eat. It is permitted to add time to Shabbat but not to take it away.

The ceremony of Havdalah

Shabbat is brought to an end at home by the ceremony of Havdalah (separation). A plaited candle is lit and then a blessing is said over a cup of wine. A spice box is passed around the family so that everyone can carry the sweetness of Shabbat into the following week.

> *Blessed are You, Hashem, our G-d, King of the universe, Who creates species of fragrance.*

A blessing is then said over the candle and is followed by a prayer:

> *Blessed are You, Hashem our G-d, King of the universe, Who separates between holy and secular, between light and darkness, between Israel and the nations, between the seventh day and the six days of labour. Blessed are You, Hashem, Who separates between holy and secular.*

Wine is drunk and what is left is used to put out the candle. Finally people wish each other 'Shavuah Tov' – 'a good week'.

AO2 skills ACTIVITIES

Read the passage on the ceremony of Havdalah. 'Celebrating the end of Shabbat is as important as marking the beginning.' Do you agree with this statement?

How do Jews celebrate Shabbat?

The next two pages will help you to:

- identify the important aspects of Shabbat
- examine how Shabbat affects Jewish life.

Jews are not allowed to drive to services at the synagogue on Shabbat.

The rules and rituals of Shabbat

There are 39 different regulations of work that cannot be done on Shabbat and these are divided into seven categories:

- *Growing and preparing food*: cooking, grinding, kneading, ploughing, reaping, selecting out, sifting, sowing, stacking sheaves, threshing, winnowing.
- *Making clothing*: combining raw materials, dyeing, removing a finished article, separating threads, sewing, sheep shearing, spinning, tearing, threading a loom, tying knots, untying knots, washing, weaving.
- *Leatherwork and writing*: cutting, erasing, flaying skins, marking out, scraping, slaughtering, tanning, trapping, writing.
- *Providing shelter*: building, demolishing.
- *Creating a fire*: extinguishing a fire, kindling a fire.
- *Work completion*: completing an object or making it useable.
- *Transporting goods*: carrying in a public place.

 **ACTIVITIES**

Talk with a partner about the things that you would find most difficult about not doing any work for a day, and why. Each of you has one minute to share your ideas.

Yom Kippur is often described as the most important day in the Jewish calendar, and is known as Shabbat Shabbaton – the Shabbat of Shabbats. People have already asked for forgiveness from relatives, friends and neighbours, but now they have to ask it from G-d.

Jews are told to observe Yom Kippur in the Torah.

> **Leviticus 16:29**
>
> *This shall remain for you an eternal decree: In the seventh month on the tenth of the month, you shall afflict yourselves and you shall not do any work, neither the native nor the proselyte who dwells among you. For on this day he shall provide atonement for you to cleanse you; from all your sins before Hashem shall you be cleansed.*

When Jews worshipped in the Jerusalem Temple, a bull and a goat were sacrificed on Yom Kippur and then the High Priest put his hands on the head of a male goat and this 'scapegoat' took all the sins of the people into the desert.

Erev Yom Kippur

After the Temple was destroyed, the scapegoat was replaced by a ceremony called **kapparah**. On Erev Yom Kippur (the evening when the festival starts) the senior man of the house brought a live chicken (or fish) indoors, waved it three times over the head of each member of the family and said 'This is our exchange, this is our substitute, this is our atonement. This rooster will go to its death, [this money will go to charity] while we will enter and go to a good, long life, and to peace.' Today many people use a handful of notes instead.

Yom Kippur was the one occasion in the year when the High Priest entered the most sacred part of the Temple, the Holy of Holies, where the Ark of the Covenant had originally been kept. In the Holy of Holies he begged for G-d to forgive the people's sins and he also spoke G-d's name.

On Erev Yom Kippur some Jewish men go to the **mikveh** (ritual bath) to cleanse themselves for the day. Yom Kippur begins at sunset. Before the festival starts there is a mitzvah meal – this means that everyone must eat it as this is a commandment. After the meal the festival candles are lit and the fast starts.

RESEARCH NOTE

Do some research about the Temples in Jerusalem. Do you think Judaism still needs the Temple?

AO2 skills **ACTIVITIES**

Write a paragraph explaining why Jews feel it is so important to ask for forgiveness at Yom Kippur.

'Everyone should spend one day of the year thinking about what they have done wrong.' Do you agree? What might a Jew say? Refer to Jewish teachings in your answers. Make sure that you have considered a variety of views.

How do Jews observe Yom Kippur?

The next two pages will help you to:

- explain the rules of Yom Kippur
- evaluate the rules of Yom Kippur
- understand the importance of Ne'ilah.

Jews wearing kittels for Yom Kippur.

The rules of Yom Kippur

On Yom Kippur many people light **yahrzeit** (year's time) candles to remember their dead relatives. Families ask for forgiveness from each other – both children and parents – and say blessings that will be sealed in the Book of Life. Yom Kippur is Shabbat Shabbaton and all the usual Shabbat rules apply. However, there are a number of extra rules that have to be observed on Yom Kippur.

- No food or drink is allowed (however, young children and people who might damage their health do not fast). There are four reasons for this fasting.
  - It shows that people wish G-d to forgive them.
  - It shows that they have self-discipline.
  - It allows people to concentrate just on spiritual things.
  - It can make someone more compassionate and understanding.
- No washing is allowed (except after using the lavatory or becoming dirty by e.g. falling over).
- No skin creams are allowed.
- No leather shoes are allowed – Jews say it would be wrong to benefit from the skin of a dead animal when they are asking G-d to be merciful to all creation.
- No sexual intercourse is allowed.

AO1
skills
ACTIVITIES

What do you think of as wrong? Write a list of activities, or thoughts, you think are wrong and need to be forgiven and explain your reasons. Do you think that we are taught what is right or wrong by school, our parents or society? Compare your ideas with those of others in your group.

All the cloths in the synagogue, including the curtains of the Ark are white to show purity. Men wear white **kippahs** and some wear a **kittel** – a full white robe like a shroud. For the evening service that begins Yom Kippur men wear their **tallitot**, which are often pure white. (This is the only occasion when men wear their tallits in the evening.)

The services of Yom Kippur

Many Jews go to the synagogue on the morning of Yom Kippur and stay there for the whole day.

There are five services on Yom Kippur rather than the usual four for Shabbat. Worship begins with the song Kol Nidrei ('All our vows'). This is followed by Al Chet, a general confession. Al Chet is a list of 44 sins. The whole congregation recites the list, using the word 'we' rather than 'I' so no one feels identified with any particular wrong-doing. Members of the congregation beat their breasts as they recite each sin.

There are many Torah readings about observing Yom Kippur and how it was celebrated at the time of the Temple.

There are also two other important readings during the services.

- Isaiah: 57–8 teaches that fasting is meaningless unless people are concentrating on their inward thoughts.
- The book of Jonah tells a story about a man being swallowed by a large fish (often assumed to be a whale), but also teaches G-d's understanding of human suffering, and that G-d is willing to forgive everyone.

Ne'ilah

The day ends with **Ne'ilah**, which means 'sealing' or 'closing'. Ne'ilah ends with the whole congregation repeating the opening verse of the Shema (see page 9).

> *Hear, O Israel, Hashem is our G-d, Hashem the One and Only.*
> *Blessed be his name, whose glorious*
> *Kingdom is for ever and ever.*
> *Blessed be his name, whose glorious*
> *Kingdom is for ever and ever.*
> *Blessed be his name, whose glorious*
> *Kingdom is for ever and ever.*
> *Hashem, he is G-d*
> *Hashem, he is G-d*
> *Hashem, he is G-d*
> *Hashem, he is G-d*
> *Hashem, he is G-d*
> *Hashem, he is G-d*
> *Hashem, he is G-d*

There is then one long final call on the shofar. People go home to eat and break their fast and to start preparing for Sukkot, which is 4 days later.

Many Jews who might not attend synagogue on Shabbat will still try to be there for Rosh Hashanah and Yom Kippur. The festivals provide an opportunity to worship and celebrate together as a community as well as an opportunity to think about life, the past and the future.

ACTIVITIES (AO2 skills)

'Fasting proves nothing.' What do you think about this statement? What might a Jew think? Give reasons for your answers.

'G-d would not want people to suffer by fasting.' What do you think? Give reasons for your answers, making sure that you have thought about Jewish teaching.

What would you personally find the most difficult thing to give up if you had to? Give reasons for your answer.

Do Jews go on pilgrimage?

The next two pages will help you to:

- examine the origins of the pilgrim festivals
- examine why sites in Israel have become important to Judaism.

Yad Vashem, Jerusalem.

The pilgrim festivals

In Judaism there are three pilgrim festivals. For each of these three events – Pesach, Shavuot and Sukkot – the instructions to celebrate them are found in the Torah. For each festival Jews travelled to Jerusalem to make offerings of each of the three harvests (barley, wheat and fruit) in the Temple. This practice became impossible with the destruction of the Temple by the Romans in 70 CE.

There are places in Jerusalem that many Jews visit on journeys that could be described as pilgrimages.

AO1 skills **ACTIVITIES**

What do you think of as a pilgrimage? Make a list of places that you would like to go to on a pilgrimage. Working in pairs, explain why you have chosen each of these places. Is there a common reason for these places?

Western Wall

All that remains at the site of the Jerusalem Temple is the Western Wall, Ha-Kotel Ha-Ma'aravi. This is part of the retaining wall of the second Temple renovated by Herod the Great. The wall dates from around the 1st century BCE. The wall itself is about 50 m long and 20 m high, with a large part being under the ground.

Today the Muslim Dome of the Rock ('Qubbat al-Sakhra') and the Al Aqsa mosque stand on the Temple Mount. Jews are asked not to walk on the Temple Mount in case, by accident, they walk on the original site of the Holy of Holies.

Many Jews visit the Western Wall to pray because it is as near as they can get to being at the original Temple. Many boys celebrate their Bar Mitzvah at the wall and people also place prayers on folded pieces of paper in the cracks of the Wall.

The rabbis taught that 'the divine Presence never departs from the Western Wall.'

Yad Vashem

Yad Vashem ('A place and a name') is just outside Jerusalem. It was established in 1953 to remember the 6 million Jews murdered by the Nazis during the Second World War. Many thousands visit Yad Vashem every year to learn about the Holocaust and to remember lost relatives.

In the Hall of Remembrance visitors can pay their respects to the dead. The floor has the names of the six death camps and 22 concentration camps that were throughout Europe. An eternal flame burns over the place where ashes brought from the various crematoria of the camps are buried.

The Children's Memorial is built in an underground cavern. Yahrzeit candles are reflected in many mirrors and the names of some of the 1.5 million Jewish children who died during the Holocaust are read aloud.

The Valley of the Communities has massive stone walls that bear the names of more than 5000 Jewish communities that were destroyed.

The Avenue of the Righteous Among the Nations was established in 1962 to honour the non-Jews who risked their lives to help Jews during the Holocaust. Over 2000 trees are planted in and around the avenue and the names of the Righteous are on plaques near the trees. The names of 19,000 more of these people are engraved on the walls of the Garden of the Righteous Among the Nations.

The Memorial to the Deportees is one of the original cattle-cars that were used to carry thousands of Jews to the death camps.

> **Isaiah 56:5**
>
> *In My house and within My walls I will give them a place of honour and renown ... eternal renown [a 'yad Vashem'] I will give them, which will never be terminated.*

ACTIVITIES

'Everyone needs to make a pilgrimage to special places.' Do you agree? Explain how a Jew might respond. Give reasons for your answer.

Why do Jews celebrate Pesach?

The next two pages will help you to:

- examine why Jews celebrate Pesach
- evaluate the importance of Pesach for Jewish life and belief.

Matzot for Pesach.

Origins of Pesach

Pesach (Passover) marks the beginning of the Jewish religious year. It takes place from 15 to 22 Nisan. No work can be done on the first and last days of the festival except for preparing food. Pesach is the first of the three pilgrim festivals and celebrates the barley harvest.

However, Pesach also recalls the night when the Angel of Death passed over the homes of the Israelite slaves living in Egypt but killed all the firstborn of the Egyptians. The hagadah says that 'every Jew should celebrate Pesach as though they had come out of Egypt themselves'.

In the Torah, Pesach is called **Chag Hamatzot**, the feast of unleavened bread. This is because at the first Pesach the Israelites ate **matzot** (hard dry bread without yeast), not the rich bread of free people. Matzot are sometimes called **lechem cherut** – the bread of freedom.

The story of Pesach is found in the book of Exodus and tells how G-d sent nine plagues on Egypt after Pharaoh had refused to let the Israelites leave. The first nine plagues were: blood, frogs, vermin, beasts, pestilence, boils, hail, locusts and darkness.

AO1 skills ACTIVITIES

Pesach is a festival that is concerned with freedom. Discuss with a partner what freedoms you think are particularly important. Make a list of these freedoms and try to put them in order of importance. Share your list with the rest of the class and see if you can agree on what is the most important freedom.

G-d then told the Israelites to prepare to leave. They were instructed to kill an 'unblemished lamb or kid'.

As the Angel of Death passed over Egypt and killed the firstborn of the Egyptians, Moses led the Israelites across the Red Sea to the desert.

The Torah instructs Jews to celebrate the festival.

Chametz

The removal of **chametz** is central to the preparations for Pesach. In the home all chametz must be removed. Chametz is not the five types of grain (barley, oats, rye, spelt and wheat) but the leaven that is produced when any of these come into contact with water for more than 18 minutes.

Matzot can be eaten because they are watched very carefully while they are being made to ensure that no water touches the flour before it is ready to be used and then for no more than eighteen minutes before they are baked.

In order to make sure that all chametz is removed, which for most Jews includes beans, corn, peas, peanuts and rice, the entire house is cleaned and all the crockery, cutlery and cooking utensils are changed or have to be soaked for several hours.

The food that could be leavened is destroyed, either by burning or by selling it to a non-Jew for the period of the festival.

Importance of Pesach

The Exodus from Egypt that is commemorated at Pesach is central to Jewish history. The Israelites were finally able to escape from the slavery of the Egyptians and return to a life of freedom in the Promised Land.

As well as celebrating freedom, the festival also remembers G-d's love for the Israelites in taking them out of slavery and helping them to live through all the problems they met during the Exodus. It demonstrates G-d's power and love for his people.

How do Jews celebrate Pesach?

A seder plate.

Erev Pesach

On the night before Pesach a special ceremony is held at home. A child searches the house by candlelight to find any remaining chametz. Usually ten pieces are hidden to remember the Ten Commandments and the Ten Plagues. The pieces are put into a bag and a statement, Kol Chamira, is made: 'All leaven and all chametz which is in my possession, which I have not seen or destroyed, nor have knowledge of shall be null, void, ownerless, and as dust of the earth.'

The next morning the last meal containing chametz is eaten, any remaining food is burnt and Kol Chamira is said again.

AO1 skills **ACTIVITIES**

What special days do you keep in your home? Are these religious or non-religious events? Why are they important to you?

The Seder

The Seder meal is a central part of the festival and is eaten on the first and second nights. Seder means 'order' and is celebrated because of an instruction in the Torah for parents to teach their children about the Exodus.

How Jews celebrate the Seder

All the readings and instructions for the Seder are in a book called the Passover Hagadah and each person at the table has a copy.

The Seder begins with questions asked by the youngest child.

- Why is this night different from all other nights?
- Why is it that on all other nights during the year we eat either bread or matzot, but on this night we eat only matzot?
- Why is it that on all other nights we eat all kinds of herbs, but on this night we eat only bitter herbs?
- Why is it that on all other nights we do not dip our herbs even once, but on this night we dip them twice?
- Why is it that on all other nights we eat either sitting or reclining, but on this night we eat in a reclining position?

Each person at the Seder must drink four cups of wine. These represent four cups and four promises. The promises can be found in Genesis 40:11–13 and Exodus 6:6–7.

There are several special objects on the Seder table:

- three matzot placed one on top of the other
- a roasted egg, which represents the sacrifices that used to be made in the Temple
- parsley – a sign of spring, new life and new hope
- a shankbone, which represents the Pesach sacrifice
- a dish of salt water – a symbol of the Israelites' tears
- lettuce or horseradish – a reminder of the bitterness of slavery
- charoset – a paste made from almonds, apples and wine, which represents the mortar used by the slaves in building.

There is also a full cup of wine for the prophet Elijah. The front door of the house is opened during the Seder in case Elijah arrives to announce the return of the Messiah.

During the reading of the story of Pesach, part of the middle matzah is hidden. This is called the **afikomen**. At the end of the meal a prize is given to the child who finds it. After the readings have finished Shulchan Orech, the festival meal, is eaten.

After eating there are more prayers and songs ending with L'Shana Ha'ba'ah Be'Yerushalayim ('Next Year in Jerusalem'). This shows the hope that eventually Jerusalem will be rebuilt as the holy city of the Jews. The Seder meal brings families and the Jewish community together with an opportunity to remember the events of the past and to 'live themselves as though they had just escaped from Egypt'.

> **Exodus 13:8**
> *And you shall tell your son in that day, saying, 'It is because of this that HASHEM acted on my behalf when I left Egypt'.*

 **RESEARCH NOTE**

Using the Internet find the answers to these questions, which are in the Passover Hagadah.

 **ACTIVITIES**

Design a short leaflet to explain the Seder to a non-Jew who has been invited to go to one.

'Festivals are really for children, not for adults.' Do you agree with this statement? Give reasons to support your answer and also consider how a Jew might respond.

Why do Jews celebrate Shavuot?

The next two pages will help you to:

- examine the origins of Shavuot
- identify how and why Jews celebrate Shavuot
- evaluate the importance of Shavuot for Jewish life and belief.

Cheesecake is traditionally eaten at Shavuot.

AO1 skills ACTIVITIES

What is the best gift that you have ever received and given? What is the worst gift you have ever received? Why do you think we give and receive gifts? Discuss these questions with the rest of the class.

Origins of Shavuot

Shavuot is the second of the three pilgrim festivals. Also known as the Feast of Weeks, Shavuot takes place on 6 Sivan and also on 7 Nisan in the diaspora (Jews who live outside Israel). In the past Jews travelled to Jerusalem to obey the mitzvah that the first fruits of the wheat harvest should be taken to the Temple. The Torah calls the festival **Chag Habikkurim**, the festival of the first fruits.

> **Leviticus 23:15–17**
>
> *You shall count for yourselves – from the morrow of the rest day, from the day when you bring the Omer of the waving – seven weeks, they shall be complete. Until the morrow of the seventh week you shall count, fifty days; and you shall offer a new meal offering to Hashem. From your dwelling places you shall bring bread that shall be waved, two loaves made of two tenth-ephah, they shall be fine flour, they shall be baked leavened; first-offerings to Hashem.*

The period from Pesach to Shavuot is called Sefirat Omer (counting the omer). An omer (3.64 litres) was used to measure barley and traditionally one omer was taken to the Temple on the 2nd day of Pesach. The counting of the omer lasts until Shavout – a period of 50 nights.

At Shavuot Jews remember G-d giving the Torah and, in particular, the Ten Commandments. This is seen as the most important event in human history.

Tradition says that the Israelites fell asleep while they were waiting for Moses to come down from Sinai with the Ten Commandments. To avoid this many Jews spend the night reading from *Tikkun Leyl Shavuot*, which is a collection of writings from the Torah and Talmud. Tradition also says that on this night heaven is open to receive prayer and study.

How Jews celebrate Shavuot

As Jews can no longer go to the Temple to offer wheat, they have special challah in their homes. These may have rungs to represent the seven spheres through which the Israelites travelled to get to Sinai; they may be square with each corner representing one of the four layers of meaning of the Torah; sometimes they are long loaves to represent the length of the Law.

> **Job 11:9**
> *Their measure is longer than the earth and wider than the sea.*

Traditionally people eat dairy foods such as cheesecake at Shavuot. This is because of the description of the Torah:

> **Song of Songs 4:11**
> *The sweetness of Torah drips from your lips, like honey and milk…*

It is also because tradition says that, until Moses spoke with G-d on Mount Sinai, the Israelites did not have the food laws and avoided meat and fish.

Synagogues and homes are decorated for the festival with flowers and greenery because Mount Sinai was covered in vegetation to celebrate the giving of the Torah.

Book of Ruth

During the synagogue service on Shavuot, the book of Ruth is read. This part of the Tenakh is about harvest and gleaning in the fields. However, it is also about a Moabite woman who, when her Israelite husband dies, stays with his family and remains true to his beliefs.

ACTIVITIES

Shavuot celebrates the giving of the Ten Commandments to Moses. Why is this so important to Jews?

'There is no real point in celebrating the pilgrim festivals without the Temple.' What do you think of this statement? How might a Jew answer this?

RESEARCH NOTE

Find out more about the story in the book of Ruth and what it says about faith and beliefs.

Why do Jews celebrate Sukkot?

The next two pages will help you to:

- examine the origins of Sukkot
- identify how and why Jews celebrate Sukkot
- evaluate the importance of Sukkot for Jewish life and belief.

Origins of Sukkot

Sukkot (festival of tabernacles) begins on 15 Tishri, 4 days after Yom Kippur, and ends on 22 Tishri. It is the third harvest festival of the year, marking the gathering in of the crops, and also celebrates the fruit harvest.

Sukkot also remembers the journey of the Israelites through the desert after they had made the Exodus from Egypt. Sukkah means a hut, booth or tabernacle. These were temporary shelters that the Israelites used in the desert. Farmers, gathering in the final harvest, lived in these temporary huts at the edge of the fields so that they did not have to travel home each night.

Sukkahs built on an apartment block.

Leviticus 23:39–40

But on the fifteenth day of the seventh month, when you gather in the crop of the land, you shall celebrate Hashem's festival for a seven-day period… and you shall rejoice before Hashem, your G-d, for a seven-day period.

Instructions for Sukkot are found in the Torah:

Leviticus 23:42–43

You shall dwell in booths for a seven-day period; every native in Israel shall dwell in booths. So that your generations will know that I caused the Children of Israel to dwell in booths when I took them from the land of Egypt; I am HASHEM, your G-d.

AO1 skills ACTIVITIES

Work with a partner and think about how you might choose to celebrate a harvest festival. Present your ideas as a spider diagram.

How Sukkot is celebrated

A sukkah is built and should only be large enough for the family who will use it. The walls can be made of anything, but the roof, the s'chah, must be natural and must be cut to be used. Therefore the branches of an overhanging tree are not suitable. The roof must also allow the light of the stars to shine through.

The sukkah is decorated inside with fruit and ushpizzin, pictures or signs showing the names of the Jewish forefathers who are each invited into the sukkah for a day: Abraham, Isaac, Jacob, Joseph, Moses, Aaron and David. Jews do not use the sukkah if it is raining because they cannot rejoice when they are suffering.

Hospitality given to non-Jews is very important during this festival as the prophet Zechariah said that one day non-Jews would travel to Jerusalem for Sukkot. Therefore Jews try to invite non-Jewish neighbours and friends to eat with them in the sukkah.

For the first two and last two days of Sukkot no work is allowed except for food preparation.

Lulav and etrog

There are two other special objects associated with Sukkot: the **lulav** and **etrog**.

> **Leviticus 23:40**
>
> *On the first day you shall take the product of hadar trees, branches of palm trees, boughs of leafy trees, and willows of the brook, and you shall rejoice before the Lord your G-d seven days.*

The lulav and etrog together are known as the Four Species. An etrog is a citrus fruit that looks like a lemon but tastes and smells very different. It must have a pittam or pistil (a hard piece of the skin of the fruit at one end) in order to be **kosher**.

The remaining three species are palm, myrtle and willow. These are put into a woven palm holder and form the lulav. Jews believe that the four species were intended to represent the final gathering in of the harvest.

On each morning of Sukkot, except the Sabbath, people put the lulav in their right hand and the etrog in their left. They put their hands together and say the blessing 'Blessed are You, Hashem, our G-d, King of the universe, Who has sanctified us with His commandments and has commanded us concerning the taking of a palm branch.'

The lulav and etrog are waved in six directions, front (east towards Jerusalem), right, back, left, up and down, which signifies G-d's power is everywhere.

RESEARCH NOTE

Find out about the various different meanings the rabbis have given to the Four Species.

AO2 skills **ACTIVITIES**

'No one can be expected to be happy eating in a hut.' What might a Jewish response be to this? What do you think? Show that you have thought about it from more than one point of view and make sure that your answer refers to Jewish teachings.

'Religious people should share their festivals with members of other religions.' Do you agree? Give reasons for your answers, showing that you have thought about it from more than one point of view.

The Jewish calendar

The next two pages will help you to:

- examine the Jewish calendar
- understand how the Jewish calendar works
- evaluate the importance of this calendar for Jewish life.

The Jewish calendar is based on the cycles of the Moon and the Sun.

ACTIVITIES

Work with a partner and think about how you might improve the calendar we use. For example, would you move some of the holidays to different times of the year? Why?

Calendars

The Jewish calendar is different from the Gregorian calendar, which is what most people in the world use for knowing the day of the month and the year.

There have always been problems with measuring time accurately. According to scientists the real length of each day is 23 hours 56 minutes and 4.1 seconds. However, to be practical, days are divided into 24 hours.

Some traditions mark time by a lunar calendar, which is based on the phases of the Moon. The day begins at sunset and the New Moon marks the start of each new month. The time between New Moons is 29.5 days. This means that there are 354 days in the lunar year.

The difficulty arises because the lunar year is 10 or 11 days shorter than the solar year, which is measured by the Sun.

Muslims use a purely lunar calendar, whereas Jews have a soli-lunar calendar.

REMEMBER THIS

Although Rosh Hashanah (New Year) takes place on the first 2 days of the 7th month Tishri, the 1st month of the Jewish year is still considered to be Nisan.

Julian calendar

In about 50 BCE Julius Caesar authorised a solar calendar. This calendar (known as Julian) had 12 months of differing lengths so that events and celebrations took place in the same season each year. In the Julian system the day begins at midnight.

The Julian calendar had leap years to correct slight inaccuracies in time-keeping but was still 11 minutes and 14 seconds short each year.

Gregorian calendar

By 1582 the calendar was 10 days out of line with the solar year and Pope Gregory XII ordered a revision to the Julian calendar. The result was the Gregorian calendar, which is what most people use now. In order to do this 10 days had to be dropped, so 3 September 1752 was followed by 14 September 1752.

In addition, one in every four years is a leap year where February has 29 days but only one in every four of the years ending in 00 are leap years: 2000 CE was a leap year but 2100, 2200 and 2300 will not be.

Pope Gregory XII.

Jewish calendar

Medieval Jewish scholars had calculated that the world was created in 3760 BCE. Therefore, the Jewish calendar starts with year 1 dated from the creation of the world in the book of Genesis. 1 Tishri 1 AM (anno mundi), is equivalent to Monday, 7 October 3761 BCE, and 1 January 2009 is 23 Tevet 5769.

The Jewish New Year starts at Rosh Hashanah in the autumn and so the date of the Jewish year can be calculated by adding 3760 or 3761 to the Gregorian year. Adding 3760 to 2009 gives 5769 AM. After Rosh Hashanah this becomes 5770 AM.

To allow for the time of the New Moon, Jewish months alternate and each month of 29 days is followed by one of 30 days. This still leaves a 12-month year of 354 days.

In order to stop the calendar losing a further 10 days every year, a leap month is added every 3rd, 6th, 8th, 11th, 14th, 17th and 19th year of each 19-year cycle. This leap month is added after the 12th month of Adar and is called Adar II or Adar Sheni.

The difficulty with a short year is that the Torah says when certain festivals must be held. Pesach (Passover) is celebrated at the time of the barley harvest in the spring and without the leap year adjustments it would soon be a long way from this date.

1st	Nisan	30 days
2nd	Iyar	29 days
3rd	Sivan	30 days
4th	Tammuz	29 days
5th	Av	30 days
6th	Elul	29 days
7th	Tishri	30 days
8th	Heshvan	29 or 30 days
9th	Kislev	30 or 29 days
10th	Tevet	29 days
11th	Shevat	30 days
12th	Adar	29 days (leap year 30 days)
13th	Adar II	29 days (leap year)

The importance of celebrating festivals at the right time became apparent when, after the destruction of the Jerusalem Temple in 70 CE, many Jews lived outside Israel and were not sure when the New Moon appeared there. Therefore, in order to make sure that everyone kept festivals at the correct time, an extra day was added to Pesach, Shavuot and Sukkot in the diaspora.

ACTIVITIES

'The important part of a festival is celebrating, not worrying about when it should be celebrated.' Do you agree? How do you think a Jew might respond to this statement?

GradeStudio

Welcome to the Grade Studio

This unit is all about how Judaism comes alive for people through celebrations, by making a special effort at certain points in the year and also by making special journeys. In this Grade Studio we will look at how you can build really good responses to AO1 and AO2 questions to ensure you give the examiner all the evidence needed to reward you with the highest level.

Examiners will be keen find out what you know about the special days and pilgrimage, but they also want you to show that you understand how these relate to the beliefs of Judaism and how they are important to individuals and to the Jewish community.

AO1

AO1 questions test what you know and how well you can explain and analyse things. Let's look at an AO1 question to see what examiners expect you to do.

Question

How do you think Jews can benefit from keeping Shabbat?   **[6 marks]**

Student's answer

A Jew can benefit from keeping Shabbat as it is an instruction to do this in their Scriptures. Also it gives them a rest day each week.

Examiner's comment

This answer is a start at answering the question, but the information is very weak. The explanation only refers to the fact that Jews are told to do this in the Scriptures but does not say why. There is no real explanation given, so this would only receive the minimum marks (Level 1).

Student's answer

A Jew can benefit from keeping Shabbat as it is an instruction to do this in their Scriptures. They do this to remember that G-d created the world in 6 days and then rested on the 7th day. Also it gives them a rest day each week when they can spend time with their family and think about G-d.

Examiner's comment

The answer gives a slightly better account of the reasons for observing Shabbat. However, it still needs to use more examples. In particular, it needs to explain how Jews might feel about observing Shabbat. This is a reasonable response but needs more development (Level 2).

Student's improved answer

A Jew can benefit from keeping Shabbat as it is an instruction to do this in their Scriptures, the Torah. They do this to remember that G-d created the world in 6 days and then rested on the 7th day. In the Ten Commandments G-d instructs the people that they must not work on Shabbat and they must keep it holy. Also, observing Shabbat gives Jews a rest day each week when they can spend time thinking about G-d and worshipping in the synagogue, as well as an opportunity to spend time with their family. Families are a very important part of Jewish life and teaching.

Examiner's comment

This is an excellent answer, which clearly explains the importance of observing Shabbat and how it might benefit a Jew (Level 3).

AO2 questions are about examining points of view and expressing your own views, using evidence and argument to support them. AO2 questions are worth 12 marks.

Examiners will use levels of response to judge the quality of your work and the best responses will have plenty of evidence to support different points of view. For AO2 there are four levels of response and for the top level the response will have a personal view supported by evidence and argument.

Question

'Festivals are the best way to learn about your religion.' Discuss this statement. You should include different, supported points of view and a personal viewpoint. You must refer to Judaism in your answer. **[12 marks]**

Student's answer

When people say that festivals are the best way to learn about your religion they are right because they are fun events and not boring. Jews might agree with this statement because festivals play a very important part in their religion and they are told to celebrate them in the Torah, their holy Scriptures.

Examiner's comment

This is a much better response. The answer gives a clear explanation of a possible Jewish view. However, it only gives one view and a personal opinion and so can only reach the top of Level 2.

Student's improved answer

I believe that when people say that festivals are the best way to learn about your religion they are right because festivals are often fun events and sometimes ordinary religious occasions can be boring especially for young children. Jews might agree with this statement because festivals play a very important part in their religion and they are told to celebrate many of them in the Torah, part of their holy Scriptures.

On the other hand, some Jews might say that although festivals are important people should learn about their religion from reading the Scriptures, listening to the teaching of the rabbis and also from their parents and family.

Examiner's comment

This is a very good answer. It gives clear explanations of two possible Jewish views as well as a personal opinion. This reaches Level 4.

These specimen answers provide an outline of how you could construct your response. Space does not allow us to give a full response. The examiner will be looking for more detail in your actual exam responses.

Remember and Reflect

AO1 Describe, explain and analyse, using knowledge and understanding

Find the answer on:

1 Explain, in one sentence, what each of the following key words means:
   a Shabbat
   b Pesach
   c Shavuot
   d Sukkot

   PAGE 29

2 Why is Shabbat important to Jews?

   PAGE 30, 31

3 Explain what Jews understand by pilgrimage.

   PAGE 40, 41

4 Why do some Jews believe it is important to visit the Western Wall and Yad Vashem?

   PAGE 41

5 Explain, giving examples, the way Pesach is celebrated.

   PAGE 44, 45

6 Explain, giving examples, the ways Sukkot is celebrated.

   PAGE 49

7 Explain, in one sentence, what each of the following words means:
   a afikomen
   b Seder
   c etrog
   d shofar
   e kittel
   f Hagadah

   PAGE 34, 39, 42, 45, 49

8 Outline three ways in which Jews might believe they benefit from observing Yom Kippur.

   PAGE 36, 37

9 Outline three ways in which Jews might believe they benefit from keeping Shabbat.

   PAGE 30, 31

10 Explain the significance of Rosh Hashanah for Jews.

   PAGE 34, 35

11 Why do Jews fast during Yom Kippur, and what does this fasting involve?

   PAGE 38, 39

12 Explain why chametz is destroyed at Pesach.

   PAGE 42–45

13 Summarise the main aspects of the Seder, explaining their significance to Jews.

   PAGE 45

AO2 Use evidence and reasoned argument to express and evaluate personal responses, informed insights, and differing viewpoints

1 Answer the following, giving as much detail as possible. You should give at least three reasons to support your response and also show that you have taken into account different opinions.
  a To be true Jews, people need to visit Jerusalem. Do you agree?
  b Do you think a Jew can celebrate Shabbat and not benefit from it?
  c Do you believe that observing Yom Kippur is helpful? Why or why not? Compare your response with that of a Jew who goes to synagogue every week and one who attends very rarely.

2 Why are festivals so important? Do you have a day that is important to you? What opportunities and challenges might Jews have that arise from the festivals they celebrate? Include examples of Jewish festivals in your answer.

3 Copy out the table, adding any other notes to the key points you think relevant, and giving your personal response with reasons.

Special event or place	Key points	What I think and why
Yad Vashem		
Yom Kippur		
Sukkot		
Shabbat		
Western Wall		
Shavuot		
Pesach		

Topic 3: Major divisions and interpretations

The Big Picture

In this Topic you will be analysing the main similarities and differences between the following Jewish groups:

• Hasidic • Orthodox • Reform • Liberal/Progressive

You will also be considering why there are different groups in Judaism and exploring how Judaism is practised in different parts of the world and how these differences might affect the lifestyles and outlooks of Jews in the modern world.

You will be exploring important issues in Judaism with reference to:

• Zionism
• the Land and State of Israel
• the Twentieth-Century Holocaust/Shoah.

What?

You will:

• develop your knowledge and understanding of the beliefs, organisation, sources of authority, worship and practices of different groups
• explore the influence of ideas, such as Zionism, and events, such as the Twentieth-Century Holocaust
• explore the challenges facing Jews in the 21st century and evaluate how the different groups respond to these challenges.

Why?

Because:

• it is important to understand the development of Judaism and have some insight into how Judaism is practised as a world-wide religion
• it is important to understand how Jewish history has influenced the religion.

How?

By:

• investigating the similarities and differences between different Jewish groups
• learning about the influence that the Twentieth-Century Holocaust, Zionism and the modern State of Israel have had on Jews
• exploring the challenges facing Judaism and evaluating how successful the responses are.

Mount Zion, Jerusalem.

GET STARTED

In pairs, on a piece of paper, create two headings: one is the town or village in which you live, the other is a different town in your area. In what ways are these places similar and different? Do they have more in common or more differences?

Major divisions and interpretations

KEY INFORMATION

- There are many different Jewish groups.

- The biggest Jewish group is the Orthodox.

- Some of the others are:
  - Hasidic
  - Reform
  - Liberal/Progressive.

- Jewish communities are found across the world.

- Jewish groups have a great deal in common, for example they accept the teachings of the Torah (see Topics 1 and 6); they use the Torah and the Talmud for help and guidance on how to live as Jews.

- They have differences and disagree on other things, for example: are the teachings of the Torah absolute or can they be reinterpreted for the 21st century? In what language should Jews worship? Can women be rabbis? Can women take part in the worship in a synagogue?

- Jews may also disagree about issues such as Zionism, the State of Israel and how they should respond to the Twentieth-Century Holocaust.

KEY QUESTIONS

KNOWLEDGE AND UNDERSTANDING

Why are there different Jewish groups?

What are the differences and similarities between these Jewish groups?

How do these groups respond to the challenges of life in the 21st century?

ANALYSIS AND EVALUATION

What are the advantages and disadvantages of having different groups within a religion?

Do the different groups within Judaism have more in common than they have differences?

How have these different groups responded to the challenges of the 20th century?

anti-Semitic Speaking or acting against Jews.

Ashkenazim Jews of Central and Eastern European origin.

Diaspora Jews living outside the Jewish State of Israel.

Gentile Person who is not Jewish.

Hasidism A religious and social movement formed by Israel Baal Shem Tov (from the 18th century onwards).

Holocaust The suffering experienced by European Jews at the hands of the Nazis, including the systematic murder of six million Jews between 1933 and 1945. Often called the Shoah.

Kibbutz Israeli collective village based on socialist principles.

kosher Foods permitted by Jewish dietary laws.

patriarchs The father and ruler of a family or tribe, in particular, Abraham, Isaac and Jacob.

Pogrom Organised attack on Jews, especially frequent in 19th- and early 20th-century Eastern Europe.

Sephardim Jews originating from Mediterranean countries, especially Spain, North Africa and the Middle East.

Shabbat Day of spiritual renewal and rest commencing at sunset on Friday, terminating at nightfall on Saturday.

Shoah See Holocaust.

Talmud Mishnah (first writing down of the Oral Tradition) and Gemara (commentary on the Mishnah included in the Talmud), collected together.

Tefillah Self-judgement. Jewish prayer and meditation.

Tenakh The collected 35 books of the Jewish Bible, comprising three sections: Torah, Nevi'im and Ketuvim (Te;Na;Kh).

Torah Law or teaching. The five books of Moses in the Scriptures.

Yishuv The Jewish community in Israel.

Zionism (Zion) Political movement securing the Jewish return to the Land of Israel.

FOR INTEREST   In 1840 the total world Jewish population was estimated at 4,500,000. By 1939 this had risen to 16,728,000. However, in 1969, 24 years after the extermination of the Holocaust, it had fallen to 13,786,000.

Who are the Hasidic Jews?

The next two pages will help you to:

- explore the origins of Hasidic Jews
- identify the particular beliefs, practices, sources of authority and styles of worship of Hasidic Jews
- reflect on the reasons for the development of the Hasidic movement.

Hasidic Jews at prayer.

AO1 skills ACTIVITIES

Answer the following questions to see how much you know about this Topic before you begin. Name two different Jewish groups. What country did Judaism originate in? What does 'pious' mean?

Origins of Hasidic Jewism

'Hasid' means 'pious'. Hasidic Judaism, which is a particular, mystical, type of life and worship, was developed in Poland in the 18th century by Israel Baal Shem Tov. 'Baal Shem Tov' means 'Master of the Good Name'. The Baal Shem Tov, as he was called, was born around 1700 in Poland and died in 1760. His original name was Israel Ben Eliezer, and he was also called Besht.

Most of the life of the Baal Shem Tov is known only from stories and legends. He was an orphan from a poor family. He did some unimportant jobs in the local synagogues but eventually married the daughter of a wealthy man and moved to the Carpathian mountains. He began to study mysticism and worked as a lime-digger. Later he became known as a healer and then worked as an innkeeper and a **schochet** (ritual slaughterer). In 1736 he moved to the village of Medzhybizh (now in the Ukraine) where he lived until his death.

The Baal Shem Tov had studied the teachings of a Kabbalistic book caled the Zohar. The book, known as 'The Book of Splendour', was written in Spain by Moses de León between 1280 and 1286. It contains teachings about a very mystical form of Judaism, including the use of astrology.

In the past most people had come to understand Judaism through studying the **Torah** (see Topics 1 and 6) and the **Talmud** (see Topic 2). In addition, the Baal Shem Tov called for a very ecstatic type of worship.

The Baal Shem Tov said that Jewish worship was too formal and should be happier. His teachings attracted many followers.

Beliefs and practices of Hasidic Jews

Hasidic teaching is based on the Talmud. It emphasises the importance of a loving relationship with G-d. Hasidic Jews believe that G-d is everywhere and that they must work to understand G-d, turn good to evil and live and act out of love for G-d and humanity.

Hasidic Jews have spiritual leaders called **tzaddikim** (saints or righteous ones). Some zaddikim are believed to have performed miracles. There are also rebbes who are community teachers.

The Hasidic community is extremely orthodox and traditional in its dress and ritual observance. The men wear black, and grow long beards and side locks. Their heads are covered at all times with skullcaps and broad-brimmed hats. Hasidic women dress modestly with long skirts and long sleeves. Married women keep their heads covered with a wig or a scarf.

Lubavitch

The Lubavitch movement is the largest single group within Hasidism. It began with the teachings of Shneur Zalman in the 18th century. The leader of the movement is known as the Habad Hasidic Rebbe.

Lubavitch aims to bring all Jewish people back to traditional practices and observance. The most famous leader of the movement was Rebbe Menachem Mendel Schneerson (1902–94).

Rebbe Menachem Mendel Schneerson.

RESEARCH NOTE

'Ecstatic' is quite a difficult concept; find out what it means when talking about religion.

ACTIVITIES

Discuss with a partner whether there are any advantages in a religion breaking up into different groups. What do you think are the disadvantages of this? Share your views with the rest of the class.

Who are the Orthodox Jews?

The next two pages will help you to:

- explain the origins of Orthodox Jewry
- understand the different origins of Sephardim and Ashkenazi Jews
- identify the particular beliefs, practices, sources of authority and styles of worship of Orthodox Jews.

The origins of Orthodox Jews

In Britain the majority of Jews are Orthodox, and under the leadership of the Chief Rabbi of the United Hebrew Congregations of the Commonwealth.

In the 19th century, when many Jews were joining the Liberal movement (see Topic 3.4), there was concern that they were leaving the traditional principles and practices of their religion.

Rabbi Samson Raphael Hirsch (1810–88) was a German theologian who thought that Jews should live in the modern world and that they should study and take part in it. However, he taught that they must still observe all the 613 mitzvot and live according to them.

Hirsch was concerned that many German Jews were turning away from Orthodoxy towards the Reform movement. The principles of Orthodox Jewry are to live strictly according to the Torah, which is a once-and-for-all revelation of G-d's words. Sometimes Orthodoxy is seen not really as a movement but as covering a whole range of traditional Jews who are not Reform, Progressive or Liberal.

Rabbi Samson Raphael Hirsch.

Sephardim and Ashkenazi Jews

Within Judaism there are two main groups that have developed in different parts of the world – the **Sephardim** and **Ashkenazi** Jews.

In 66 CE the people of Israel revolted against Rome and its rulers, who were in charge of Israel. This revolt continued until Jerusalem was finally taken back by the Romans in 70 CE. At this time the Temple in Jerusalem was destroyed and the Jews were expelled from the city. Jews no longer had a focal point for their religion. The Jews who left Israel became known as **Diaspora** Jews.

AO1 skills **ACTIVITIES**

Discuss with a partner. What does 'orthodox' mean? Now look the word up in a dictionary and check the definition. Were you right or wrong? On your own, make a list of ten things that you think are orthodox and ten that are unorthodox. Check with your partner – do you agree?

Sephardi

After leaving Israel, many Jews eventually lived under Muslim rule. Jews in Spain reached many positions of power in the 10th and 11th centuries. The type of Judaism that developed in this area became known as Sephardic. 'Sephardin' comes from the modern Hebrew name for Spain (Sepharad).

The origins of the word 'Sepharad' are unclear, though there is one reference in the Tenakh that is sometimes taken to refer to Spain:

> **Obadiah 1:20**
> *And that exiled force of Israelites [shall possess] what belongs to the Phoenicians as far as Zarephath, while the Jerusalemite exile community of Sepharad shall possess the towns of the Negeb.*

A North African Sephardi woman in traditional dress.

Sephardi Jews have their own language called Ladino or Judaeo-Spanish. It is a mixture of Hebrew and Spanish, but also contains words from Arabic, French, Greek and Turkish.

The Sephardi Jews follow a form of Judaism developed in Babylon rather than the Palestinian practices of the Ashkenazim.

Today there are approximately 700,000 Sephardi Jews, who make up only 17 per cent of world Jewry but are half of the population of Israel.

Ashkenazi

Jews who lived in other parts of Christian Europe were called Askenazim or Ashkenazi, from 'Ashkenaz', the Hebrew for 'Germany'. Ashkenazi Jews moved eastwards from Germany into Poland during the 15th and 16th centuries. Some emigrated to North America and Israel during the 19th and 20th centuries. This name probably comes from the name Ashkenaz, the great-grandson of Noah.

> **Genesis 10:1–3**
> *These are the descendants of the sons of Noah – Shem, Ham, and Japheth; sons were born to them after the Flood. The sons of Japheth – Gomer, Magog, Madai, Javan, Tubal, Meshech, and Tiras. The sons of Gomer – Ashkenaz, Riphath, and Togarmah.*

The language of Ashkenazi Jews was Yiddish, a type of medieval German with Slavonic and Hebrew words. Many Ashkenazi Jews became money lenders for Christians who believed there was a ban on borrowing money at interest. However, they were often expelled from the countries when they were no longer needed.

In some areas such as northern Europe and North America, most Orthodox Jews are Ashkenazi, whereas in southern Europe, North Africa and the Middle East they tend to be Sephardic. Approximately 85 per cent (10.2 million) of all Jews are Ashkenazim.

AO2 skills **ACTIVITIES**

'Everyone who belongs to a religion must live and worship in the same way.' Discuss this statement. Give your own opinions and also what you think a Jew might say.

Who are the Reform Jews?

The synagogue of the Mickve Israel Reform congregation in Savannah, Georgia, USA, built in 1876.

The origins of Reform Judaism

In the 18th century the Haskalah or Jewish Enlightenment movement wanted to change Jewish life so that Jews could be better integrated into **Gentile** society. They also wanted to improve Jewish education so that it included secular studies as well as Hebrew and Jewish history.

Moses Mendelssohn (1729–86) believed that Jews should not keep themselves separate from everyone else and argued that there should be equal rights for Jews.

Mendelssohn was concerned that with greater freedom in Germany many Jews were deserting their religion.

From 1810, Israel Jacobson (1768–1828), who is often considered to be the founder of Reform Judaism, introduced changes in the synagogue services: the services were shortened and sermons were preached in the vernacular (German) so that all the congregation could understand them. Before this time sermons had always been in Hebrew. Prayers in German were used as well as the traditional ones in Hebrew and choirs and organs were introduced into worship. Some prayers were changed to remove references to animal sacrifices in the Jerusalem Temple. The first synagogue to change its service was the Hamburg Temple in 1818.

AO1 skills **ACTIVITIES**

Why do you think it might be important that religions never change? Discuss with a partner and then with your class.

FOR INTEREST

Moses Mendelssohn was the first Jew to translate the five books of the Torah, the Psalms and other sections of the Tenakh into German.

Beliefs and practices of Reform Judaism

In most Reform communities men and women sit together to worship, whereas in Orthodox congregations they sit separately (see page 93). These Jews did not want to break away from tradition but argued that these changes were compatible with traditional Judaism. The movement did not stress the need for a return to Jerusalem. They did say that there was a need for ethical living and for a belief in the benefits of human progress.

The movement began to hold conferences to discuss beliefs and practice. The first were in Brunswick (1844), Frankfurt (1845) and Breslau (1846). The issues considered included easing the rules about work on the Sabbath and also those on marriage and divorce.

Reform Judaism has developed and changed since the 19th century. This has happened because Reform Jews do not believe that there is only one way of understanding Jewish belief and the Law.

The first Reform community in Britain was founded in 1840. Today, about 15 per cent of British Jews belong to Reform synagogues, which are represented by the Reform Synagogues of Great Britain (RSGB).

The Reform movement developed differently in Britain and America from the way it did in Germany.

The West London Synagogue.

In Britain the West London Synagogue accepted the Bible as the word of G-d but rejected the Talmud as being written by humans. These Reform congregations also accepted biblical criticism (the idea that the Bible can be discussed and may contain errors or show evidence that it was written down by humans even though it is the word of G-d). They also held a belief in 'Progressive Revelation'. This meant that G-d could still reveal things to humanity, and that belief and understanding could therefore develop and change.

In America Reform Judaism is the largest Jewish denomination. It accepts gay couples and same-sex commitment ceremonies. Reform rabbis also bless mixed-faith marriages and recognise those people who have a Jewish father but a non-Jewish mother as being Jewish. Some of these beliefs are also accepted in Britain, but Reform Judaism has some differences in belief and practice around the world.

AO1+AO2 skills ACTIVITIES

Most Orthodox Jewish men can be recognised by their clothes and beards. Most Reform Jews do not wear distinctive clothing. Do you think that it is better for people to be recognised as a follower of a religion or not? Give reasons for your answer.

Who are the Liberal and Progressive Jews?

The next two pages will help you to:

- explain the origins of Liberal and Progressive Jewry
- identify the particular beliefs, practices, sources of authority and styles of worship of Liberal and Progressive Jews
- reflect on the reasons for the development of the Liberal and Progressive movements.

The origins of Liberal and Progressive Jews

The terms 'Liberal' and 'Progressive Judaism' can be confusing as in some parts of the world they are used to describe Reform Judaism and other movements. The movement began in the United Kingdom, on 18 October 1902, when 300 people met in the Wharncliffe Rooms at the Great Central Hotel, London.

This meeting had been called by Lily Montague (1873–1963), the first woman to play an important role in Progressive Judaism, who, with others, was concerned about the many Jews who were leaving their religion.

This was the first meeting of the Jewish Religious Union, which later became the Union of Liberal and Progressive Synagogues. There was a mixed male and female choir who sang in English and Hebrew accompanied by a harmonium. The service was conducted by an Orthodox rabbi, Simeon Singer, and the sermon was given by Claude Montefiore (1858–1938).

Rabbi Julia Neuberger DBE.

Montefiore was a theologian who had studied at Oxford. He believed that scholars had shown that the Torah was not written by Moses, was not all by one person and had mistakes in it. However, he believed that Jews should follow the Law as they understand it for themselves.

The original idea of the Jewish Religious Union was simply to add to existing services to make them more meaningful for people, but this was rejected by the Chief Rabbi. The West London Synagogue (see Topic 3.3) offered to hold the meeting but at that time would not allow men and women to sit together, which the Union wanted.

ACTIVITIES

Explain why Jews have formed different groups. Give at least two different reasons for this.

The first Liberal and Progressive synagogue was established in a rented building in Hill Street, London. The first rabbi was an American, Israel Mattuck.

Many changes were proposed, such as the moving of Sabbath services from Saturday to Sunday and a rejection of Zionism (see page 68). The Liberal and Progressive movement believed that Jews should live in the world and did not need to re-establish Israel as a Jewish state.

The synagogue moved to a new building in St John's Wood Road, London, in 1925. The World Union for Progressive Judaism was founded in 1926 at an international conference held at the new synagogue.

In 1942 the movement changed its name to 'The Jewish Religious Union for the Advancement of Liberal and Progressive Judaism' and, in 1944, to 'The Union of Liberal and Progressive Synagogues'.

Jews at the El Ghriba synagogue in Djerba, Tunisia, lighting candles to celebrate Lag B'Omer (the 33rd day of the Omer) (see p. 47).

Liberal and Progressive Judaism today

In Britain, Liberal and Progressive rabbis are trained at the same college as rabbis in the Reform tradition. However, the two movements have never fully united. The Union now has 30 congregations and a thriving youth movement.

The Union of Liberal and Progressive Synagogues (ULPS) has a very radical approach to social issues and a liberal theology that shows respect for all humanity.

The ULPS has made a statement of Affirmations. These include:

- the view that children of mixed marriages – that is, those between a Jew and a non-Jew – are to be treated alike, regardless of whether the mother or the father is the Jewish parent, and considered Jewish if so brought up
- welcoming into the congregation all who have a good claim to be regarded as Jewish, regardless of marital status or sexual orientation
- that there is no sex segregation in their synagogues: women and men may lead services, become rabbis and hold any synagogue office
- the equal status of boys and girls in religious education
- recognising that there are loving, committed relationships other than marriage between a man and a woman
- recognising the right of Jewish same-sex couples, with and without children, to receive equal treatment in all areas of congregational life, including the right to celebrate their partnerships with a Service of Commitment conducted by a rabbi.

This is part of a ULPS prayer for human rights (right).

ACTIVITIES

'The first responsibility of all religious people should be to take care for the poor.' Do you agree? Give reasons to support your answer. What might a Jew say in response to this?

> *Eternal G-d, help us to recognise Your image*
> *In the face of every human being,*
> *And to accept fully in our hearts*
> *The responsibility we bear for others.*
> *Teach us to walk in all Your ways:*
> *As You provide food enough for all*
> *Let us ensure that all have food to eat.*
> *As You provide materials to clothe the naked,*
> *Let us ensure that all have clothing and shelter.*

What is Zionism?

What is Zionism?

The word '**Zion**' has been used for over 3000 years. Originally it meant the hill, Mount Zion, on which the Jerusalem Temple was built. Later the word came to mean Jerusalem and eventually Israel.

Zionism is a movement that aims to bring together all the Jews of the **Diaspora** and return them to the Promised Land of Israel. The beginning of this hope for a return to Israel was in the 6th century BCE when Jews were held captive in Babylon. Also, after the destruction of the Temple in 70 CE, there were always small Jewish groups who stayed in Israel.

In the second half of the 19th century many anti-Semitic parties began to appear in Germany and Austria. Following the assassination of the Russian czar Alexander II in 1881 anti-Jewish **pogroms** spread across the country. Many of the Russian Jews emigrated to the United States and some went to Palestine.

The word 'Zionism' was first used in 1890 by the Austrian Jewish philosopher Nathan Birnbaum. In 1896, Theodor Herzl published a book called *Der Judenstaat* (*The Jewish State*). He said that it was time to establish Eretz Israel (the Land of Israel) as a Jewish state. Not all Jews support the ideas of Zionism and many Orthodox Jews believe that Jews will not return to Israel as a Jewish country until the Messiah has returned.

The first Zionist Congress was held in Basel in 1897. This produced a document called the *Basel Programme*. The goal of the Programme was the creation 'for the Jewish people of a home in Palestine secured by public law'. At this congress the World Zionist Organization (WZO) was set up.

Herzl made an unsuccessful attempt to get support from Turkey to establish a Jewish state. He then tried the British government.

Children working on a kibbutz.

AO1 skills ACTIVITIES

Make a list of religions that you have studied at school. For each one explain what you think its homeland is and why.

Development of Zionism in the 20th century

Britain considered the possibility of establishing a Jewish state in Uganda, which at the time was governed by the United Kingdom. However, this was turned down by the seventh Zionist Congress in 1905.

Zionists had different ideas about a new Jewish state. Some stressed the importance of Israel becoming a cultural centre for Judaism as well as a spiritual one. Others talked about a 'religion of labour' where the people and the land worked together towards a successful country. Religious Zionists aimed to strengthen Judaism by returning people to their homeland.

Before any further progress was made over the establishment of an official homeland, Zionists began to establish Kibbutzim (collective farms) in Palestine.

In 1917, during the First World War (1914–18), the Balfour Declaration promised to establish a 'national home for the Jewish people' in Palestine. This was in return for Jewish co-operation with Britain during the war. However, after the war nothing further happened.

In 1929 the Jewish Agency was set up to provide financial support for the Jews who lived in Palestine. Palestine was ruled by Britain from 1920 to 1948.

In 1939 the British government ended its commitment to Zionism and said that there would be a Palestinian state established within ten years. Those Arabs living in Palestine were protected because now only 75,000 Jews were going to be allowed to emigrate before 1944. After that date any Jewish immigration would depend on the agreement of the Arabs.

An Extraordinary Zionist Congress of 1942 demanded the establishment of a Jewish Democratic Commonwealth in Palestine.

By the end of the Second World War (1939–45) the Yishuv (Jewish settlement) had grown from 50,000 to 600,000 people. Many of these were people who had escaped from the fascist dictators of Europe, including Adolf Hitler in Germany and Benito Mussolini in Italy.

A major difficulty in Palestine was how the Jews were to live alongside the mainly Arab population. Some Zionists suggested that there should be a joint Arab–Jewish state.

However, some others, led by David Ben-Gurion (the first prime minister of Israel) said that the Jewish state must be established before there could be any negotiations with the Arabs.

Since the creation of the State of Israel, the World Zionist Organization (WZO) has used its energies in assisting Jews to move to Israel, supporting particularly the struggle of Jews in the former USSR who wished to emigrate. It provides support for Israel but has little to do with Israeli politics.

ACTIVITIES

'Every religion has the right to a homeland.' Do you agree? Give reasons to support your answer. What might a Jew say in response to this?

What is the Land of Israel?

The next two pages will help you to:

- explore what is meant by 'the Land of Israel'
- consider what Jews understand by the biblical idea of the Land of Israel.

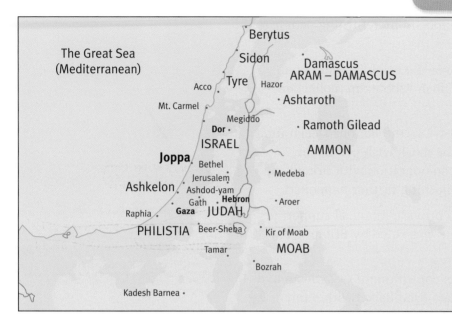

The Land of Israel.

AO1 skills **ACTIVITIES**

Is there a particular place that is very important to you? Try to think of one and then explain to your partner why it is important. Compare the places you have both thought of and in what ways they are important.

The Promised Land

The idea of the Land of Israel or the Promised Land is found in Genesis.

> **Genesis 12:7**
>
> *The Lord appeared to Abram and said, 'I will assign this land to your heirs.' And he built an altar there to the Lord who had appeared to him.*

> **Genesis 13:14–15**
>
> *And the Lord said to Abram, after Lot had parted from him, 'Raise your eyes and look out from where you are, to the north and south, to the east and west, for I give all the land that you see to you and your offspring forever.'*

The patriarchs lived in the land as 'sojourners' – people who are in a place for a short time. However, the promise of the land for the Israelites is repeated again and again in the book of Genesis.

After the Exodus from Egypt (see page 16) the Israelites had new hope of returning to the land. When G-d spoke to Moses at the Burning Bush he said that he had come to recuse the Israelites from the Egyptians and take them back to Canaan, the land flowing with milk and honey (Exodus 3:8).

The Promised Land is established when Joshua brings the Israelites back; it then becomes the land ruled by David and Solomon.

> **2 Samuel 3:10**
>
> '…to transfer the kingship from the House of Saul, and to establish the throne of David over Israel and Judah from Dan to Beer-sheba.'

> **1 Kings 5:1**
>
> Solomon's rule extended over all the kingdoms from the Euphrates to the land of the Philistines and the boundary of Egypt.

From the 9th to the 7th centuries BCE Israel was invaded by Assyrians and Babylonians and the people were then exiled in other countries:

> **Psalm 137:1 and 4**
>
> By the rivers of Babylon,
> there we sat,
> sat and wept,
> as we thought of Zion.
> How can we sing a song of the Lord
> on alien soil?

 **FOR INTEREST**

'By the rivers of Babylon' was a famous song at the end of the 20th century. Try to find out more about it.

The prophets said that the Israelites would eventually go back to the Promised Land:

> **Isaiah 27:12–13**
>
> And in that day, the Lord will beat out [the peoples like grain] from the channel of the Euphrates to the Wadi of Egypt; and you shall be picked up one by one, O children of Israel!
> And in that day, a great ram's horn shall be sounded; and the strayed who are in the land of Assyria and the expelled who are in the land of Egypt shall come and worship the Lord on the holy mount, in Jerusalem.

 **ACTIVITIES**

Work in small groups and choose one of the events above. Explain why the event is important to Jewish history. Discuss this statement: 'G-d promised the land to the Jews and they should live there.' Explain your opinions.

This return took place under Zerubbabel, Ezra and Nehemiah in the 5th century BCE.

The Jews were finally driven out of the land in 70 CE after the failed uprising against the Romans.

For Judaism it has always been an aim to return to the land that G-d originally promised to the patriarchs.

What is the State of Israel?

The next two pages will help you to:

- explore the establishment of the State of Israel
- reflect on the challenges that the State of Israel has brought to the people who live there.

The establishment of the State of Israel

The events of the Twentieth-Century Holocaust (see Topics 3.8 and 3.9) convinced Jews of the need for an independent Jewish state and, in 1944, Menachem Begin led the Irgun Zvai Leumi (National Military Organization) in a revolt against British rule in Palestine.

ACTIVITIES

Discuss with a partner what you would be prepared to fight for and why. Share your thoughts with the class. What are the most common and least common reasons for people's decisions about this?

David Ben-Gurion (1886–1973), chairman of the executive committee of the Jewish Agency for Palestine, passed the resolution to declare the independence of Israel on 14 May 1948, by a vote of 6 to 4 (for further information, see the Wikipedia website). There was opposition from both sides of the Jewish political spectrum. In the Israeli declaration of independence, he stressed that the nation would 'uphold the full social and political equality of all its citizens, without distinction of race, creed or sex'. British rule ended at midnight on 14 May 1948.

As soon as the state was established, Ben-Gurion ordered the disbandment of all resistance groups, to be replaced by the Israel Defence Forces (IDF). Ben-Gurion became prime minister on 25 February 1949. Apart from the period from 1954 to 1955, he remained in post until 1963. The establishment of the state had been helped by sympathy in the West for the suffering of the Holocaust, by the influence of American Jews on President Truman and by the difficulties Britain was having in ruling Palestine. Ben-Gurion would not allow the Zionist leaders in the diaspora to have any influence over Israel's affairs and said that, following the establishment of the state, the only purpose of Zionism was to encourage Jews to settle in Israel.

There are now two basic Zionist principles: the safety of the State of Israel, and the right of any Jew to settle in Israel under the Law of Return. While the Promised Land is an idea with its basis in the Jewish Scriptures, the present-day State of Israel is an independent country.

The boundaries of the Promised Land found in the Jewish Scriptures cover a much larger area at the eastern end of the Mediterranean than is contained by the modern State of Israel. The State of Israel is not a religious Jewish state, although religion does have a strong influence on politics in the country.

Challenges to the State of Israel

The modern history of Israel has involved many conflicts with the Muslim Arabs who lived in the country before the Jewish state was established. In 1967, during the Six-Day War, Israel took control of East Jerusalem, the Gaza Strip, the West Bank region of Jordan, the Golan Heights – an area of south-western Syria – and the Sinai Peninsula of Egypt.

The Yom Kippur War took place between 6 and 26 October 1973 in an Arab attempt to win back the land taken by Israel in 1967. In 1982 the Sinai Peninsula was returned to Egypt and in 1994 the Gaza Strip and the West Bank town of Jericho came under Palestinian self-rule.

In 2005 Israeli settlers left the Gaza Strip. Although Jerusalem is the country's capital, this is not recognised by the United Nations and many countries have their embassies in Tel Aviv–Yafo instead.

The population of Israel is about 6.5 million. This includes East Jerusalem, the Golan Heights and Israeli settlers in the West Bank. Jews represent approximately 76 per cent of the total population. The remainder are Muslims (15.9 per cent), Christians (1.8 per cent) and Druze (1.7 per cent). The final 4.6 per cent of the population are outside these groups (2007 figures).

RESEARCH NOTE

Find out who the Druze are.

The destruction caused by Israeli bombing in Beirut, the capital of Lebanon, on 14 August 2006.

ACTIVITIES

'Peoples of different religions should always live together in peace.' Discuss this statement. Give reasons to support your answer and consider Jewish responses. Explain why this has been difficult to achieve in Israel.

The Twentieth-Century Holocaust/ Shoah (1)

The next two pages will help you to:

- explore the origins of the Twentieth-Century Holocaust
- explain why the Holocaust took place.

Anti-Jewish signs in Nazi Germany.

The origins of the Twentieth-Century Holocaust/ Shoah

Anti-Semitism is any activity of hatred (speech or behaviour) directed against the Jewish people, regardless of whether they are religious. The Romans refused citizenship of the Empire to most Jews on the grounds of their beliefs and worship. From the 4th century CE, Jews were regarded by many Christians as 'Christ killers'. The spread and domination of Christianity made anti-Semitism universal and the suppression of the Jews simple. During the crusades, thousands of Jews were massacred and later they were placed in ghettos and forced to wear distinctive clothing so that they were easily recognised.

The Spanish Inquisition, established by the pope in 1478 CE at the request of King Ferdinand V and Queen Isabella I, was designed to deal with the 'problem' of Marranos, Jews who, under pressure, had insincerely converted to Christianity. Tens of thousands of Jews were executed and the remaining were driven out of Spain in 1492.

For centuries there were outbreaks of anti-Semitism and pogroms throughout Europe. Although Jews were given equal status in Germany in 1871, many people still hated and mistrusted them.

In 1933 the National Socialist (Nazi) government made anti-Semitism official policy. This policy was based on the theory that people of Aryan stock such as white Christians were superior to Semitic people such as the Jews. Adolf Hitler, the chancellor of Germany, wished to create a 'Master Race'. This would contain only Aryan people, tall with blonde hair and blue eyes.

AO1 skills ACTIVITIES

Anti-Semitism is a type of racism. Identify some examples of racism that exist in the 21st century.

Many of the Jews in Germany were in very powerful positions and Hitler argued that they were the main cause of all Germany's problems and must be stopped.

When the Nazis came to power, they passed laws that excluded Jews from legal protection. Over time their property was seized by the government and they were sent to concentration camps where they were tortured and made to carry out slave labour. Many were then taken to extermination camps for death. This started on a small scale but was carried out nationwide in 1938.

The Final Solution

Hitler devised a theory called the Final Solution. He attempted to have all the Jews in Europe collected together in camps in Germany and Poland. There were 22 camps, including Auschwitz-Birkenau, Ravensbruck, Sobibór, Thereseienstadt and Treblinka, and here the Jews were gassed. Six million Jews, together with millions of other 'undesirables' such as gypsies, homosexuals, mental defectives, Jehovah's Witnesses, Mormons, Slavs and Communists were also executed.

In autumn 1941 the Nazis began the deportation of all Jews from occupied Europe to the east (Poland and Russia) for extermination.

However, Hitler was not successful and after the defeat of the Third Reich by the Allies (Britain, the former USSR and the United States of America) in 1945, Judaism began to grow once more.

Rabbi Hugo Gryn (1930–96).

Jewish responses about forgiveness

Jews believe that they should always forgive other people who are sorry for what they have done, but that they cannot forgive on behalf of others. When he was asked if he could forgive the Nazis for the Holocaust the late Rabbi Hugo Gryn, who had been in Auschwitz, said that only G-d could forgive their crimes. Judaism believes that peace must always be sought before fighting.

> **Psalm 34:15**
> *Turn from evil and do good, seek peace and pursue it.*

Although Judaism is not a pacifist religion and believes that there are occasions when war has to take place, it does believe that peace is the highest good.

This is from a letter from Jewish philosopher Martin Buber, which was sent to M.K. Gandhi:

❝ *For I cannot help withstanding evil when I see that it is about to destroy the good. I am forced to withstand the evil in the world as the evil within myself. I can only strive not to have to do so by force. I do not want force. But if there is no other way of preventing the evil destroying the good, I trust I shall use force and give myself up into G-d's hands.* **❞**

ACTIVITIES

'Racism is always wrong.' Discuss this statement. Give reasons for your response and explain how a Jew might respond to the statement.

The Twentieth-Century Holocaust/ Shoah (2)

After the Holocaust

Although the governments of the world are now largely opposed to any idea of anti-Semitism, outbreaks still occur. There have been incidents of vandalism and defacing of Jewish monuments and synagogues in France, Germany, Britain and the USA. At the Second Vatican Council (1962–65), the Roman Catholic Church abandoned the teaching that all Jews were responsible for the death of Christ and condemned all genocide and racism.

In the former USSR, anti-Semitism survived because Judaism and Zionism were seen as the enemies of communism. Education for Jews continued to be strictly limited and emigration was effectively impossible. Conditions improved slightly with the break-up of the USSR, but anti-Semitic protests still continue.

After 1945 some of the Jewish property that had been taken by the Nazis was returned to the survivors or their heirs. However, many Jews and Jewish organisations said that the return of this money and property was completely out of proportion to what had happened during the Holocaust.

In the 1950s the government of West Germany reached agreement with the Conference on Jewish Material Claims against Germany that it would pay over £500 million to the State of Israel and towards rebuilding the Jewish communities in Europe that had been destroyed.

After 1990, when East and West Germany were reunified, negotiations were started to obtain extra compensation for survivors of the Holocaust. Much of the money from Jewish property that had been taken by the Nazis had been placed in Swiss bank accounts. In 1998 an agreement was also made with the Swiss banks for about £850 million to be paid in compensation.

The next two pages will help you to:

- explore some of the issues facing Judaism after the Twentieth-Century Holocaust
- reflect on Jewish responses to the Twentieth-Century Holocaust.

The main gate of Auschwitz II – Birkenau.

 **ACTIVITIES**

Working with a partner, make a list of the reasons why you might stop trusting someone that you have known for a long time. What would they have to do for you to not trust them anymore? Share your thoughts with the class.

What did Jews think after the Holocaust?

It was an inevitable reaction to the extermination of such a large proportion of world Jewry during the Second World War that many Jews began to question their faith.

Some Jews felt that the members of the Nazi party who were still alive after the Second World War should be brought to trial for their crimes. Simon Wiesenthal (1908–2005), who had spent 4.5 years in the concentration camps at Janowska, Kraków-Płaszów and Mauthausen-Gusen, dedicated most of his life to bringing these people to justice.

Some Jews felt that the relationship between the Jews and G-d – the covenant relationship – was broken, and that G-d had let the Jews down by allowing the Holocaust to happen. Some Jews simply had a complete loss of faith. Others found that it strengthened their faith in the belief that only a stronger and more faithful Judaism could provide a solution.

Some people believe that the experience of the Holocaust means that people need to think about the way Judaism should be followed in the future. The views of post-Holocaust Judaism are sometimes expressed as:

- G-d was in Auschwitz
- G-d was not in Auschwitz
- G-d died in Auschwitz.

Richard Rubenstein (b.1924 – a major teacher and writer in the American Jewish community) argued that the Holocaust could not be what G-d wanted to happen, but that if this was the case then G-d must be dead. Emil Fackenheim (1916–2003) said that the most important thing for Jews to do was to avoid giving Hitler a victory by losing their faith. He said that no one would ever understand why the Holocaust happened, as only G-d can know that. However, the existence of the State of Israel shows that G-d is still looking after the Jews.

Ignaz Maybaum (1897–1976 – one of the leading Jewish theologians of the 20th century) said that the Holocaust was part of G-d's plan and that Judaism has now entered a new period.

Eliezer Berkovits (1908–92 – a rabbi and teacher within Modern Orthodox Judaism) argued that the death of 6 million Jews showed their faith in G-d and proves that G-d exists. G-d allowed the Holocaust to happen but did not cause it. The Holocaust shows that people do have free will, which is an essential part of being human. Albert Friedlander (1927–2004 – a Reform rabbi and radical Jewish leader) said that Jews would have to change their opinion of G-d and of humanity and find new ways of believing.

ACTIVITIES

'It is time to forget the Twentieth-Century Holocaust and forgive.' Do you agree with this statement? Explain the reasons for your answer and include Jewish opinions.

GradeStudio

Welcome to the Grade Studio

In this Grade Studio we will look at the longer AO1 responses required for part (d) of the question, which is worth 6 marks. Part (d) of each question will be marked according to levels. For AO1, there are three levels. A good response to part (d) will be well organised, contain relevant knowledge and will have a full, well-developed explanation. If required, you should analyse the Topic, which means you might make a comparison between two aspects of the Topic.

Graded examples for this topic

AO1

AO1 questions test what you know and how well you can explain and analyse things. Let's look at an AO1 question to see what examiners expect you to do.

Question

Why are there different groups within Judaism? **[6 marks]**

Student's answer

Jews do not agree on everything so over time they have formed themselves into different groups for worship.

Examiner's comment

This answer is a start at answering the question, but the information is very weak. The explanation only refers to the fact that Jews might disagree but does not say why. There is no real explanation given, so this would only receive the minimum marks (Level 1).

Student's answer

Jews do not agree on everything so over time they have formed themselves into different groups for worship. In particular, they disagree about how much they should keep themselves separate and how much they should mix with non-Jews.

Examiner's comment

This answer gives a slightly better account of the reasons for the existence of different groups. However, it still needs to use more examples. In particular it needs to give more examples of the reasons for the differences. This is a reasonable response at Level 2 but needs more development.

Student's improved answer

Jews do not agree on everything so over time they have formed themselves into different groups for worship. In particular they disagree about how much they should keep themselves separate and how much they should mix with non-Jews. Jews have different opinions about whether they must follow all the mitzvot and some feel that they should adapt more to the world around them. There are also different opinions about the use of Hebrew, whether men and women can sit together in the synagogue and whether women can be rabbis.

Examiner's comment

This is an excellent answer, which clearly explains some of the reasons for the existence of different Jewish groups (Level 3).

AO2 questions are about examining points of view and expressing your own views, using evidence and argument to support them. AO2 questions are worth 12 marks.

Examiners will use levels of response to judge the quality of your work and the best responses will have plenty of evidence to support different points of view. For AO2 there are four levels of response and for the top level the response will have a personal view supported by evidence and argument.

Question

'The Twentieth-Century Holocaust proves that G-d does not exist.' Discuss this statement. You should include different, supported points of view and a personal viewpoint. You must refer to Judaism in your answer. **[12 marks]**

Student's answer	Examiner's comment
The Twentieth-Century Holocaust was a disaster for Judaism. Six million Jews were killed and many people gave up believing in G-d as a result. I think that after an event like this no one could be expected to believe in G-d, even though I don't believe in G-d myself.	This is a much better response. The answer gives a clear explanation of a possible Jewish view. However, it only gives one view and a personal opinion and so can only reach the top of Level 2.

Student's improved answer	Examiner's comment
The Twentieth-Century Holocaust was a disaster for Judaism. Six million Jews were killed and many people gave up believing in G-d as a result. However, there are many Jews who feel that, although the Holocaust was a terrible event, people must not give up belief in G-d. Some people say that at least the Holocaust led in some ways to the establishment of the State of Israel. I think that after an event like this no one could be expected to believe in G-d, even though I don't believe in G-d myself.	This is a very good answer. It gives clear explanations of two possible Jewish views as well as a personal opinion. This reaches Level 4.

These specimen answers provide an outline of how you could construct your response. Space does not allow us to give a full response. The examiner will be looking for more detail in your actual exam responses.

Remember and Reflect

AO1 Describe, explain and analyse, using knowledge and understanding

Find the answer on:

1 Give three examples of Jewish religious groups.
→ PAGE 58

2 Name three things all these groups have in common.
→ PAGE 58

3 Name two things some of these groups disagree on.
→ PAGE 58

4 What do the following words mean?
  a *pious*
  b *mysticism*
  c *Orthodox*
  d *Progressive*
→ PAGE 60, 62, 66

5 Who was the founder of Hasidic Judaism?
→ PAGE 60

6 Where did Reform Judaism begin?
→ PAGE 64

7 When did Liberal/Progressive Judaism begin?
→ PAGE 66

8 Explain what is meant by anti-Semitism.
→ PAGE 74

9 Explain some of the differences between Ashkenazi and Sephardi Jews.
→ PAGE 62, 63

10 What is Yiddish?
→ PAGE 63

11 What is Ladino?
→ PAGE 63

12 What are the origins of the Twentieth-Century Holocaust or Shoah?
→ PAGE 74

13 Name three of the Nazi concentration camps.
→ PAGE 75

14 What is the word Nazi short for?
→ PAGE 74

15 Who was the leader of the Third Reich?
→ PAGE 75

16 Explain the origins of Orthodox Judaism.
→ PAGE 62

17 Which was the first synagogue to follow Reform practices in its services?
→ PAGE 64

18 Explain Zionism.
→ PAGE 68

19 What was the Balfour Declaration?
→ PAGE 69

20 In which country did Britain want to establish a Jewish state?
→ PAGE 69

21 Explain what is meant by the 'Promised Land'.
→ PAGE 70

AO2 Use evidence and reasoned argument to express and evaluate personal responses, informed insights, and differing viewpoints

1 Answer the following, giving as much detail as possible. You should give at least three reasons to support your response and also show that you have taken into account different opinions.

a Do you think Judaism needs a homeland?

b All Jews believe in the same G-d, so they should all worship in the same way. How far do you agree?

c Jewish groups have more in common than they have differences. Do you agree?

d Women and men should worship together. Do you agree?

Topic 4: Places and forms of worship

The Big Picture

In this Topic you will learn about:

- what places of worship might look like and what they show about what Jews believe
- key features of Jewish places of worship, their meaning and purpose
- ways that Jews express their beliefs through different forms of worship.

What?

You will:

- develop your knowledge and understanding of the purpose and use of Jewish places of worship
- explain how worship expresses Jewish beliefs
- make links between these beliefs and ideas and what you think/believe.

Why?

Because:

- worship is an important feature of Jewish belief and one that affects the lives of Jews and those of their communities
- exploring the meanings behind the ways in which Jews worship will enable you to apply and extend your understanding of Jewish beliefs
- understanding that our beliefs affect our actions helps you to consider the meaning of other people's actions as well as your own.

How?

By:

- identifying and describing the key features of Jewish places of worship
- connecting the use and purpose of places of worship with Jewish beliefs
- evaluating your own views about these beliefs.

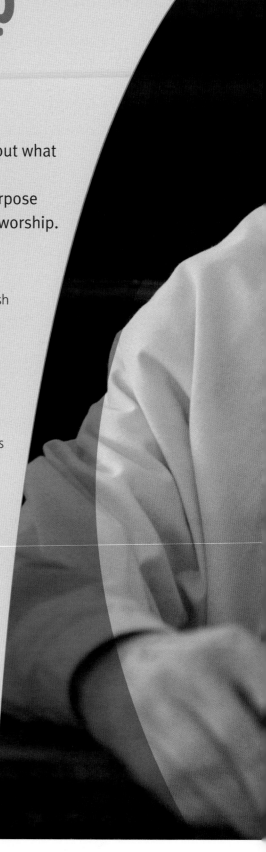

A Jew praying in a synagogue.

GET STARTED

'People can worship G-d anywhere; they don't need to go to special buildings.' Do you agree or disagree? Give reasons. Do a survey to find out what people think about this question and why.

Places and forms of worship

- Synagogues serve many purposes as well as being used for worship.

- Jews may worship in a synagogue but can also worship at home.

- Jews hold their services on Shabbat from Friday evening until Saturday evening.

- Most Jewish worship is very similar, although there are differences between groups such as Orthodox, Reform, Liberal and Progressive.

- Most services are liturgical, which means that they follow a set pattern.

- One of the most important aspects of Jewish worship in a synagogue is the reading from the Torah scrolls.

- Prayer is a common feature of worship both at home and in a synagogue.

- The leader of the Jewish community is called a rabbi, but services are often led by a chazan or cantor.

- The Jewish Scriptures (the Tenakh and Talmud) are used by Jews in their public and private worship.

- Jews have particular religious dress that is symbolic.

KEY QUESTIONS

KNOWLEDGE AND UNDERSTANDING

Why is the Jewish place of worship called a synagogue?

When were synagogues first used?

Why are they important to Jews?

How do Jews use the synagogue?

ANALYSIS AND EVALUATION

If Jews can worship at home, why do they need a synagogue?

Why are there no pictures of G-d or the prophets in a synagogue?

Why do different groups of Jews worship differently?

Aron Hakodesh The focal point of the synagogue, containing Torah scrolls.

Bet ha knesset House of assembly.

Bet ha midrash House of study.

Bet ha tefilla House of prayer.

bimah Raised platform primarily for reading the Torah in the synagogue.

kippah, yamulkah or capel Head covering worn during prayers, Torah study, etc. Some followers wear it constantly.

kittel Plain white robe worn by Jewish men, particularly on Yom Kippur.

kosher Foods permitted by Jewish dietary laws.

Magen David Star of David.

menorah Seven-branched candelabrum that was lit daily in the Temple.

mezuzah A scroll placed on doorposts of Jewish homes, containing a section from the Torah and often enclosed in a decorative case.

mitzvot Commandment. The Torah contains 613 mitzvot.

Ner Tamid Eternal light. The perpetual light above the Aron Hakodesh.

rabbi A Jewish teacher. Often the religious leader of a Jewish community.

Sefer Torah Torah scroll. The five books of Moses handwritten on parchment and rolled to form a scroll.

Shabbat Day of spiritual renewal and rest commencing at sunset on Friday, terminating at nightfall on Saturday.

synagogue or shul Building for Jewish public prayer, study and assembly.

tallit Prayer shawl. Four-cornered garment with fringes.

tefillin Small leather boxes containing passages from the Torah, strapped on the forehead and arm for morning prayers on weekdays.

tzizit Fringes on the corners of the tallit. Also commonly refers to the fringed undervest worn by some Jewish males.

FOR INTEREST The oldest synagogue to which there is reference dated from between 70 and 50 BCE and was near Jericho. The oldest fragments of a synagogue are in Egypt and date from the 3rd century BCE.

Where and why do Jews worship?

The next two pages will help you to:

- understand the origins and purpose of a synagogue
- consider the different uses of a synagogue
- evaluate whether special places of worship are necessary.

The Ohel Jakob synagogue in Munich, Germany.

What is a synagogue?

Although a synagogue is a place of public worship for Jews, the main place of worship is in the home. The name synagogue is from the Greek 'σθναγφγηω' and means a meeting or an assembly.

In Hebrew a synagogue is called: Bet ha tefilla (house of prayer), Bet ha knesset (house of assembly) or Bet ha midrash (house of study). In Yiddish the word 'shul' (from the German 'Schule', 'school') is also used for a synagogue. In America, some Jews call their synagogue a Temple.

The synagogue provides a community centre for Jews for prayer, study and meetings. This has been particularly important where Jews live in small communities within a larger non-Jewish town or city.

AO1 skills ACTIVITIES

From memory, write down as many names of places of worship as you can think of. Next, for each one, state which religion it is used by. Compare your list with a partner and correct the lists if necessary. How many different names can you find?

The origins and purpose of a synagogue

Following the destruction of Solomon's Temple in 586 BCE Jews met temporarily at the Bet ha midrash to study the Scriptures. Some people believe that the first mention of a synagogue is in the book of Ezekiel.

> **Ezekiel 11:16**
>
> *Thus said the Lord G-d: I have indeed removed them far among the nation and have scattered them among the countries, and I have become to them a diminished sanctity (synagogue) in the countries.*

The Talmud says that this verse refers to a small portable synagogue, which the Jews used when they were in exile in Babylon. The earliest known synagogue was in Egypt in the 3rd century BCE. There is a 1st-century Greek inscription that mentions teaching in a synagogue in Palestine. During the 1st century BCE there were synagogues in Asia Minor, Babylonia, Egypt, Greece, Palestine and Rome. The earliest ruins of synagogues are at Masada and Herodium and both date from the 1st century CE.

In Palestine there is a 1st-century BCE Greek inscription that mentions the synagogue being used for teaching. These synagogues were possibly used by local communities while their priestly representatives were in Jerusalem.

An inscription in a 1st-century synagogue in Palestine says that Theodotus, son of Vettenos, built a synagogue 'for the reading of the Torah and teaching of the commandments and also built the hospice and chambers and water installations for lodging needy strangers'.

The first Temple in Jerusalem was built by King Solomon in the 10th century BCE. This was destroyed by the Babylonians in 586 BCE. Rebuilding started in 520 BCE. This second Temple was repaired by Herod the Great around 20 BCE. When the Jerusalem Temple was destroyed in 70 CE Jews could no longer make animal sacrifices and these were replaced by prayer. By this time most communities had synagogues where prayer services were held and these now became centres for Jewish life and worship.

With the end of sacrifices priests were no longer needed and their place as community leaders were taken by rabbis. The word 'rabbi' means 'my master' and has been used since the 1st century BCE as a title of respect for Jewish leaders.

Uses of the synagogue

Since the destruction of the Temple synagogues have continued the traditions of teaching and worship from the Bet ha midrash and Bet ha tefilla, but have also been important community centres for Jewish life.

Synagogues also house the **cheder** (room), which is a religious school for Jewish children.

ACTIVITIES

'A synagogue is essential for a Jewish community.' What do you think? How might a Jew respond to this? Give reasons for your answers, showing that you have thought about it from more than one point of view.

What does a synagogue look like?

Many synagogues are very plain buildings from the outside. Often the only indication of what their function is the symbol of a Magen David (Shield or Star of David). Another possible symbol is a menorah (seven-branched candlestick).

There is no particular reason for synagogues being plain buildings and there are some that are not. However, their origins in the portable synagogues of Babylon and the village structures that were of secondary importance to the Temple may be part of the reason. In Eastern Europe many synagogues were converted or used by very poor communities so there would have been little money to spend on unnecessary architectural features.

Also, many synagogues continue to be plain because of a desire not to draw attention to themselves for fear of anti-Semitic attacks.

Some synagogues may have stained-glass windows but these will not have any pictures of people in them because of the teachings of the second commandment, which forbid idol worship.

ACTIVITIES

Find pictures of synagogues and other religious buildings. Make a list of differences and similarities. Try to explain to your partner why these similarities and differences might be important.

> **Exodus 20:4**
>
> *You shall not make for yourself a sculptured image, or any likeness of what is in the heavens above, or on the earth below, or in the waters under the earth.*

Magen David

The earliest example of a Magen David or hexagram dates from the 7th century BCE and was found in Sidon.

Inside the synagogue at Capernaum, which was built in the 2nd or 3rd century CE, the hexagram is found next to a pentagram and a swastika. All three are here used as forms of decoration.

The Star of David in a Jewish burial ground.

By the beginning of the 6th century CE the Magen David is called the 'Seal of Solomon'. For a long time the two names 'Shield of David' and 'Seal of Solomon' were both used for the symbol of the hexagram.

The first official use of the Magen David is not found until 1354 when the Holy Roman Emperor Charles IV allowed the Jewish community in Prague to have its own flag. This flag became known as 'King David's flag' and had a Magen David or hexagram symbol on it.

In the 21st century, the Magen David is the symbol on the flag of Israel but the symbol of the country is the seven-branched menorah.

The wall that faces Jerusalem is where the Ark is placed, so often the synagogue may have an entrance hall that has a door facing Jerusalem. The synagogue must also have windows.

RESEARCH NOTE

Find out more about the religious use of the swastika.

> **Daniel 6:11**
>
> *[Daniel] ... went to his house, in whose upper chamber he had had windows made facing Jerusalem, and three times a day he knelt down, prayed, and made confession to his God, as he had always done.*

A stained-glass window showing a man reading from the Sefer Torah.

בן שלש עשרה למצות

AO2 skills **ACTIVITIES**

'Synagogues should be large and impressive buildings to show that Jews are proud of their religion.' How far do you agree with the comment? Give reasons for your answer and make sure that you give Jewish responses as well.

Inside a synagogue (1)

The next two pages will help you to:

- identify some of the main features of the interior of a synagogue
- examine how these features reflect Jewish belief.

The Aron Hakodesh of the Great Synagogue Ades of the Glorious Aleppo Community in Jerusalem.

What does the interior of a synagogue look like?

Inside, most synagogues have very similar features. Most importantly, there are no pictures or statues in a synagogue in accordance with the teachings of the second of the Ten Commandments.

Exodus 20:4–5a

You shall not make yourself a carved image nor any likeness of that which is in the heavens above or on the earth below or in the water beneath the earth. You shall not prostrate yourself to them nor worship them, for I am Hashem, your G-d – a jealous G-d…

The wall facing Jerusalem is called the mizrach. Here is a cupboard called the Aron Hakodesh, the Holy Ark.

AO1 skills ACTIVITIES

Often when people go into a religious building they say that it 'feels different'. This feeling is often called the numinous or Holy Other. What places give you this sort of feeling? Make a list and then try to explain to your partner why you have chosen them.

The Aron Hakodesh

The Aron Hakodesh represents the Holy Ark that the Israelites built at G-d's instruction to contain the tablets of stone on which were written the Ten Commandments. When the Israelites returned to the Promised Land after the Exodus from Egypt, the Ark was placed in the Holy of Holies in the Jerusalem Temple. The Holy of Holies (Kadosh Hakadashim) was the inner sanctuary of the Jerusalem Temple at the west end of the building. The inside was kept in total darkness. It was hidden by a veil and entered only once a year on Yom Kippur by the High Priest.

> **Exodus 25:10–22**
>
> *They shall make an ark of acacia wood, two and a half cubits long, a cubit and a half wide, and a cubit and a half high. Overlay it with pure gold – overlay it inside and out – and make upon it a gold molding round about. Cast four gold rings for it, to be attached to its four feet, two rings on one of its side walls and two on the other. Make poles of acacia wood and overlay them with gold; then insert the poles into the rings on the side walls of the ark, for carrying the ark. The poles shall remain in the rings of the ark: they shall not be removed from it. And deposit in the Ark [the tablets of] the Pact which I will give you.*
>
> *You shall make a cover of pure gold, two and a half cubits long and a cubit and a half wide. Make two cherubim of gold – make them of hammered work – at the two ends of the cover. Make one cherub at one end and the other cherub at the other end; of one piece with the cover shall you make the cherubim at its two ends. The cherubim shall have their wings spread out above, shielding the cover with their wings. They shall confront each other, the faces of the cherubim being turned toward the cover. Place the cover on top of the Ark, after depositing inside the Ark the Pact that I will give you. There I will meet with you, and I will impart to you – from above the cover, from between the two cherubim that are on top of the Ark of the Pact – all that I will command you concerning the Israelite people.*

The Ark contains the Sefer Torah (Torah scrolls). These scrolls are wound onto two wooden rollers called the **Etz Chaim** – the Trees of Life. The scrolls have velvet covers and an ornate breastplate (tas), which represents the breastplate that was worn by the High Priest of the Jerusalem Temple. On the top of the rollers are silver crowns (keter) and bells that are called rimmonim (pomegranates). The front of the Ark is covered with a **parochet** or curtain.

Above or to the sides of the Ark, there are two tablets bearing the first two words of each of the Ten Commandments. Also, in front of the Ark may be the verse 'Know before whom you are standing.' This comes from the Talmud.

Above and in front of the Ark burns the Ner Tamid, the eternal or perpetual light. This represents the lamp that burnt in the Temple in Jerusalem. On or above the parochet are the Lions of Judah. Finally, there is a crown (Keter Torah). Jews believe that the Torah is the crowning glory that G-d gave to the world.

> **Genesis 49:9**
>
> *Judah is a lion's whelp; On prey, my son, have you grown. He crouche, lies down like a lion, Like the king of beasts, who dare rouse him?*

 **ACTIVITIES**

'The Jewish Scriptures should be in a book so that they are easier to read.' Do you agree with this statement? Give reasons for your answer and include Jewish responses.

Inside a synagogue (2)

The next two pages will help you to:

- identify some of the main features of the interior of a synagogue
- examine how these features reflect Jewish belief.

A menorah.

The main features of the interior of a synagogue

There is often a seven-branched candlestick (menorah) embroidered on the covering of the Ark. This menorah represents the candlestick that stood in the Jerusalem Temple.

Exodus 25:31–32

You shall make a Menorah of pure gold, hammered out shall the Menorah be made, its base, its shaft, its cups, its knobs, and its blossoms shall be [hammered] from it. Six branches shall emerge from its sides, three branches of the Menorah from its one side and three branches of the Menorah from its second side.

AO1 skills **ACTIVITIES**

Try to explain why you think people have special buildings to worship in.

The seven-branched menorah in the photograph is different from the nine-branched one used at the festival of Hanukkah and called a Hanukiah.

The reader's desk (shulchan) is placed immediately in front of the Ark. This is because, in the Talmud, the prayer leader is called 'yored lifnei ha-tevah' he who goes down before the Ark.

The Torah itself is read from the bimah, sometimes called the almemar. This is a raised platform that is sometimes surrounded by a safety rail. It stands in the centre of the synagogue so that the entire congregation can hear and see the reading. Before being read the scrolls are removed from the Ark and then carried in procession around the synagogue. They are then undressed and placed on the bimah. At the end of the Torah reading they are re-dressed and returned directly to the Ark.

While the scrolls are being read, the reader follows the line of script with a silver pointer shaped like a hand with a finger pointing forward. This is called a yad and means that the scrolls are not touched by hand. When the scrolls are dressed the yad is hung over the top of the rollers.

In Orthodox synagogues, men and women sit separately for worship. There is a mehitzah – a partition screen, usually lattice, which separates the women's area from the men's.

Sometimes the women sit in an upstairs gallery (Weibershul). This is based on teachings in the Talmud that explain how the men and women sat separately for the festivals.

As women do not play any part in the synagogue worship they can watch and listen to the service without being in the men's section.

In most Progressive synagogues, men and women now sit together and may also both take part in the services.

Beyond the prayer hall

As well as the central prayer hall there may be many other rooms in a synagogue. Remember that a synagogue is Bet ha knesset (house of assembly) and Bet ha midrash (house of study), as well as Bet ha tefilla (house of prayer).

There will be offices, meeting rooms, a kitchen and a room for the cheder (religious school). Jewish children are usually taught at the cheder on Sunday mornings but there may also be classes in the evenings during the week. They learn about Jewish history and beliefs as well as reading Hebrew, particularly in preparation for Bar Mitzvah.

Finally, most Orthodox synagogues will have a ritual bath called a mikveh.

RESEARCH NOTE

Find out why a Hanukiah has nine branches.

AO2 skills **ACTIVITIES**

'The Ten Commandments are very old and Jews should put pictures of G-d and the prophets in the synagogue to make it more interesting.' How far do you agree with the comment? Give reasons for your answer and make sure that you give Jewish responses as well.

Religious dress (1)

The next two pages will help you to:

- explain some of the different articles of Jewish religious dress
- consider the importance of religious dress for Jews.

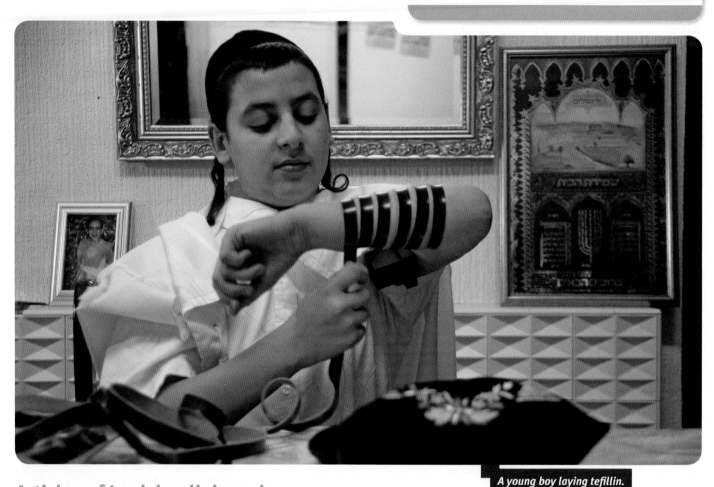

A young boy laying tefillin.

Articles of Jewish religious dress

There are five main articles of Jewish religious dress that are worn by men:

- kippah, yamulkah or capel
- tefillin
- tallit
- tzizit or tallit katan
- kittel.

Kippah, yamulkah or capel

This is the skullcap often worn all the time by Orthodox Jewish men. It can be made of almost any material and may be embroidered. It is a reminder that the wearer is always in the presence of G-d. It is always worn for prayers and for Torah study.

AO1 skills ACTIVITIES

Work with a partner. What do you think it is worth wearing special clothes for? Explain why you might do this.

Tefillin or phylacteries

In accordance with Exodus 13:9, Jewish men 'lay tefillin' before morning prayer on weekdays (tefillin are not worn on the Sabbath).

> ### Exodus 13:9
> *And this shall serve you as a sign on your hand and as a reminder on your forehead – in order that the Teaching of the Lord may be in your mouth – that with a mighty hand the Lord freed you from Egypt.*

Tefillin are two small, black, leather boxes with thongs, the hand-tefillah shel yad and the head-tefillah shel rosh. They both contain a piece of parchment on which is written the Shema (see page 9): Deuteronomy 6:4–9, 11:13–21 and Numbers 15:37–41.

> ### Deuteronomy 6:4–9
> *Hear, O Israel! The Lord is our G-d, the Lord alone. You shall love the Lord your G-d with all your heart and with all your soul and with all your might. Take to heart these instructions with which I charge you this day. Impress them upon your children. Recite them when you stay at home and when you are away, when you lie down and when you get up. Bind them as a sign on your hand and let them serve as a symbol on your forehead; inscribe them on the doorposts of your house and on your gates.*

The shel yad is put on first with the bayit or box on the biceps muscle of the left arm (the right arm for a left-handed person). The strap is wound around the arm seven times. Then the shel rosh is tied on the forehead above and between the eyes with a knot at the nape of the neck. The strap of the shel yad is then tied around the hand.

Tallit

The tallit or prayer shawl is worn every day for morning prayer. It is a long fringed shawl (usually white) with blue or black stripes. The fringes make eight strands with five knots at each corner. These fringes are called tzizit and in the Hebrew numbering system the letters of tzizit are equal to 600:

600 + 8 (strands) + 5 (knots) = 613

These represent the 613 commandments in the Torah.

> ### Numbers 15:37–41
> *The Lord said to Moses as follows: Speak to the Israelite people and instruct them to make for themselves fringes on the corners of their garments throughout the ages; let them attach a cord of blue to the fringe at each corner. That shall be your fringe; look at it and recall all the commandments of the Lord and observe them, so that you do not follow your heart and eyes in your lustful urge. Thus you shall be reminded to observe all My commandments and to be holy to your G-d. I the Lord am your G-d, who brought you out of the land of Egypt to be your G-d: I, the Lord your G-d.*

The tallit is only worn during evening prayer on Yom Kippur. When a Jewish man dies he is often buried in his tallit. The tassels are cut off to show that he is no longer bound by the mitzvot.

ACTIVITIES

'Providing that you pray it does not matter what you wear.' What do you think? Give reasons, using evidence from this Topic and your own knowledge to justify your answer.

Religious dress (2)

The next two pages will help you to:

- explain some of the different articles of Jewish religious dress
- consider the importance of religious dress for Jews.

ACTIVITIES

Make a list of the items in the last two pages. Without looking back at the pages or your notes, explain why each one is important for Jews.

Because of a commandment not to cut the corners of their hair, some Jews allow the hair in front of their ears to grow down into payes.

Articles of Jewish religious dress

Tzizit or tallit katan

This is an undergarment shaped like a tabard with fringes that are visible under the shirt. In Hasidic communities (as well as some others) it is always worn as an outer garment.

Kittel

The kittel is a plain white robe worn on Yom Kippur and Hoshanah Rabbah and also used as a burial shroud – a simple garment that shows equality for all in death. In some communities it is also worn by a bridegroom at his wedding.

Because of a commandment not to cut the corners of their hair, some Jews allow the hair in front of their ears to grow down into payes or pyres (Hebrew 'pe'ot').

Deuteronomy 22:12
You shall make tassels on the four corners of the garment with which you cover yourself.

Leviticus 19:27
You shall not round off the side-growth on your head, or destroy the side-growth of your beard.

Women's religious dress

There are no particular dress requirements for women other than to dress modestly. However, some Orthodox women wear a sheitel to cover their hair. This may be a scarf or hat but in more recent times, it is often a wig.

Meah Shearim

Meah Shearim is one of the oldest neighbourhoods in west Jerusalem, having been established in 1874.

The population is very Orthodox. Traditions in dress may include black frock coats and on Sabbaths, festivals and special occasions such as weddings, black or fur-trimmed hats for men. Women wear long-sleeved, modest clothing and some wear thick black stockings all year long, including summer. Married women wear headscarves.

There are 'modesty' signs at every entrance to the area:

> **To women and girls who pass through our neighbourhood.**
> **We beg you with all our hearts.**
> **Please do not pass through our neighborhood in immodest clothes.**
> **Modest clothes include: closed blouse, with long sleeves.**
> **Long skirt, no trousers, no tight-fitting clothes.**
> **Please do not disturb the sanctity of our neighbourhood.**
> **And our way of life as Jews committed to G-d and his Torah.**

ACTIVITIES

'To treat men and women differently is simply wrong.' What do you think? Give reasons, using evidence from this Topic and your own knowledge to justify your answer.

'Modesty' signs at one of the entrances to Meah Shearim.

Worship in the synagogue

The next two pages will help you to:

- understand Jewish worship in the synagogue
- evaluate the importance of this worship for Jews.

Shabbat worship at the Pestalozzistraße Synagogue in Berlin-Charlottenburg, Germany.

Synagogue service

The synagogue service and prayers are printed in a book called a Siddur. Each Shabbat the sermon is given by the rabbi (a Jewish teacher). The rabbi is not a priest – there have been no priests in Judaism since the Temple was destroyed in 70 CE. A rabbi is chosen by the congregation as the leader and teacher of the local community.

A group of rabbis forms the Beth Din (the Jewish religious court) for the area. The Beth Din is responsible for all issues concerned with Jewish law, especially food. It also has jurisdiction over issues such as divorce and conversion.

During the service, the readings and singing will be led by the chazan or cantor, who is an official of the synagogue.

ACTIVITIES

Working with a partner explain to each other what you both think are the most important parts of worship. Write down those that you agree on and those on which you disagree. Share your findings with the class.

For any service to take place there must be a minimum of ten adult males (minyan). During the service each man will wear a kippah and, at a morning service, a tallit. Any male who has reached Bar Mitzvah age can form part of a minyan.

During the service the congregation say prayers, join in the singing and may make formal responses to parts of the service. They may also be 'called up' to read from the scrolls. This is seen as a great honour.

Practices and beliefs of the synagogue service

Tallitot are worn at the evening service only on Yom Kippur. In an Orthodox synagogue the service will be almost entirely in Hebrew. In Reform and Liberal/Progressive synagogues parts of the service will be in English.

The service consists mainly of prayers and the central reading of the Torah, the whole of which is read at Sabbath services during the course of each year. Services are also held on Mondays and Thursdays with Torah readings.

There are services for Shabbat in the synagogue on Friday and Saturday. Generally the morning service follows this form:

1   Morning blessings of thanksgiving
2   Blessings and psalms, ending with the Song of Moses (Exodus 15:1–19)
3   The Shema (Deuteronomy 6:4–9, 11:13–21, Numbers 15:37–41)
4   Amidah or standing prayer
5   Torah service when the scrolls are carried around the synagogue and the week's portion of the Torah is read. This is followed by a reading from the Prophets, the **Haftarah** ('completion')
6   Musaf – additional service for the Sabbath
7   Aleynu – praises to G-d, then psalms and hymns
8   In some communities: Kiddush, when the congregation say blessings over wine and challot (singular: 'challah') which are then shared.

Synagogue worship is, in some ways, one of the great strengths of Judaism. Particularly in areas where there are very few Jews, it provides an opportunity for the community to come together at least once a week and so, as well as worship, it can help to support and strengthen the faith of believers.

MUST THINK ABOUT!

Rabbis are certified but, although this gives them a title, there is no suggestion that it conveys any special powers on them such as in Christianity.

Exodus 15:1–3

Then Moses and the Israelites sang this song to the Lord. They said: I will sing to the Lord, for He has triumphed gloriously; Horse and driver He has hurled into the sea. The Lord is my strength and might; He is become my deliverance. This is my God and I will enshrine Him; The God of my father, and I will exalt Him.
The Lord, the Warrior –
Lord is His name!

Deuteronomy 6:4–5

Hear, O Israel: HASHEM is our G-d, HASHEM is the One and Only. You shall love HASHEM, your G-d, with all your heart, with all your soul, and with all your resources.

Amidah paragraph 1

Blessed are You, HASHEM, our G-d and the G-d of our forefathers, G-d of Abraham, G-d of Isaac, and G-d of Jacob; the great, mighty, and awesome G-d, the supreme G-d, Who bestows beneficial kindnesses and creates everything, Who recalls the kindnesses of the Patriarchs and brings a Redeemer to their children's children, for His Name's sake, with love.

ACTIVITIES

'Informal worship is more important than special services in the synagogue.' What do you think? Give reasons, using evidence from this Topic and your own knowledge to justify your answer.

Worship in the home

The next two pages will help you to:

- explain how Jews worship at home
- understand the use of the mikveh
- evaluate the importance of the home in Jewish life and worship.

A mezuzah at the door of a synagogue.

AO1 skills ACTIVITIES

Someone is visiting your home. What might the objects in your house tell them about you and your family? Are any of these objects religious? What do you think the visitor would learn about you and your family by looking around your home?

How Jews worship at home

The Jewish home is a very special place and central to Jewish worship and prayer life. Friday evening Shabbat ceremonies take place at home, as does Havdalah. Also, many of the festivals are celebrated in the home, particularly Pesach and Sukkot. In a Jewish home, reminders of faith and beliefs are around at all times.

The kitchen will have been specially equipped for cooking kosher food. A small cylinder is fixed to the top of the right-hand doorpost as you enter a room. It contains the mezuzah, a piece of parchment on which is written the Shema. Every door except for the bathroom has a Mezuzah. As they pass through the door many Jews touch the mezuzah and take their fingers to their lips.

There will be candlesticks and a Kiddush cup for Shabbat and many Jews have a small piece of wall which is unfinished and undecorated as a reminder of the destruction of the Jerusalem Temple.

Deuteronomy 6:7

You shall teach them thoroughly to your children and you shall speak of them while you sit in your home, while you walk on the way, when you retire and when you arise

Prayer

Male Jews are required to pray three times a day.

There are three daily periods of prayer:

- evening: ma-ariv
- afternoon: mincha
- early morning: shacharit.

All Jewish prayers are said facing east, towards Jerusalem. As well as formal prayers Jews may also say spontaneous prayers, which are simple thanks to G-d for something that happens, such as seeing a beautiful view.

Jews will study the Tenakh at home individually as well as use it to teach their children and to discuss the text with each other.

Passages from the Siddur are read before and after meals.

> ### Grace after meals – first blessing – for nourishment
> *Blessed are You, HASHEM, our G-d, King of the universe, Who nourishes the entire world, in His goodness – with grace, with kindness, and with mercy. He gives nourishment to all flesh, for His kindness is eternal. And through His great goodness, we have never lacked, and may we never lack, nourishment, for all eternity. For the sake of His Great Name, because He is G-d Who nourishes and sustains all, and benefits all, and He prepares food for all of His creatures which He has created. Blessed are You, HASHEM, Who nourishes all. Amen.*

Purity and the use of the mikveh

The laws of **Niddah** (purity) play a very important part in Jewish life.

Mikveh

Every synagogue should have a ritual bath or mikveh. This is a pool of natural water in which people can bathe to be ritually pure:

> ### Ezekiel 36:25
> *Then I will sprinkle pure water upon you, that you may become cleansed; I will cleanse you from all your contamination and from all your idols.*

An ancient mikveh at Masada, Israel.

There may also be a separate mikveh in which cooking pots can be made pure for kosher cooking:

> ### Numbers 31:22–23
> *Only the gold and the silver, the copper, the iron, the tin, and the lead, everything that comes into the fire – you shall pass through the fire; but it must be purified with the water of sprinkling; and everything that would not come in the fire, you shall pass through the water.*

Every mikveh must contain at least 40 se'ah (between 250 and 1000 litres) of natural water. This could be stream or rain water.

Women must visit the mikveh after the end of their monthly period to cleanse themselves before they can resume normal sexual relationships with their husbands. The mikveh is also used for converts and some Orthodox Jewish men use it regularly and, in particular, before Yom Kippur.

ACTIVITIES

'For Jews, the home is more important than the synagogue.' Do you agree with this statement? Give reasons for your answer and include what a Jew might say in response.

GradeStudio

Welcome to the Grade Studio

In this Grade Studio we will look at the longer AO1 responses required for part (d) of the question, which is worth 6 marks. Part (d) of each question will be marked according to levels. For AO1, there are three levels. A good response to part (d) will be well organised, contain relevant knowledge and will have a full, well-developed explanation. If required, you should analyse the Topic, which means you might make a comparison between two aspects of the Topic.

Graded examples for this topic

AO1

AO1 questions test what you know and how well you can explain and analyse things. Let's look at an AO1 question to see what examiners expect you to do.

Question

Explain why the mikveh is important for Jewish life.   **[6 marks]**

Student's answer

> The mikveh is a bath to make things clean.

Examiner's comment

This is a start to responding to the question, but the answer is very weak. The explanation only refers to the obvious. There is no real explanation. This response is only Level 1.

Student's improved answer

> The mikveh is a special ritual bath. It is used according to the laws of Niddah (purity). After her monthly period a woman has to go to the mikveh before she can start having sexual relationships with her husband again. Some men also go to the mikveh. The mikveh is used for converts and also there is a special mikveh that is used for making pots and pans kosher.

Examiner's comment

This is an excellent answer. The candidate could have limited their answer to just some examples and perhaps explained them in more depth, but this is another way of answering the question where all the uses of the mikveh are considered.

AO2 questions are about examining points of view and expressing your own views, using evidence and argument to support them. AO2 questions are worth 12 marks.

Examiners will use levels of response to judge the quality of your work and the best responses will have plenty of evidence to support different points of view. For AO2 there are four levels of response and for the top level the response will have a personal view supported by evidence and argument.

Question

'Worship in the home is more important than worship in the synagogue.' Discuss this statement. You should include different, supported points of view and a personal viewpoint. You must refer to Judaism in your answer. **[12 marks]**

Student's answer

The synagogue is where the Torah scrolls are kept and where people go to pray so it is obviously more important than the home for worship.

I agree with this view because you should go to a special place to worship G-d.

Examiner's comment

This is a better response. The answer gives an explanation of a possible Jewish view. However, it only gives one view and an undeveloped personal opinion and so can only reach Level 2.

Student's improved answer

The synagogue is where the Torah scrolls are kept and where people go to pray on Saturdays as well as other days of the week. However, the home is very important because in some ways all Jewish life is worship and people spend more time at home than they do in the synagogue. Also many special events, such as festivals and Shabbat meals, take place at home so you could argue that the home is much more important than the synagogue for worship.

I agree with this view because I do think that you should go to a special place to worship G-d. However, I can see that for Jews in particular there are many special events that make the home very important.

Examiner's comment

This is a very good answer. It gives clear explanations of two possible Jewish views as well as personal opinions. This reaches Level 4.

These specimen answers provide an outline of how you could construct your response. Space does not allow us to give a full response. The examiner will be looking for more detail in your actual exam responses.

Remember and Reflect

AO1 Describe, explain and analyse, using knowledge and understanding

Find the answer on:

1 Explain, in one sentence, what each of the following key words means:
   a synagogue
   b tallit
   c kittel

   PAGE 85

2 Why is the synagogue important to Jews?

   PAGE 86, 87

3 Explain what is meant by Niddah.

   PAGE 101

4 Explain what is meant by spontaneous prayer.

   PAGE 101

5 What is the Ner Tamid and why is it important?

   PAGE 91

6 Explain, giving examples, the different types of religious dress worn by Jews.

   PAGE 94–97

7 Explain, giving examples, what happens in a Shabbat morning service.

   PAGE 98, 99

8 Explain, in one sentence, what each of the following words means:
   a menorah
   b Magen David
   c parochet

   PAGE 88, 91, 92

9 Explain why worship in the home is important for Jews.

   PAGE 100

10 Suggest reasons why synagogues are often very plain buildings.

   PAGE 88

AO2 Use evidence and reasoned argument to express and evaluate personal responses, informed insights, and differing viewpoints

1 Answer the following, giving as much detail as possible. You should give at least three reasons to support your response and also show that you have taken into account opposite opinions.

a *Jews must find it difficult to go to the synagogue on Saturdays when other people are out enjoying themselves. Do you agree?*

b *Do you think Jewish forms of worship are still relevant in today's world?*

c *Do you think that people need to wear special clothes to worship G-d? Why or why not?*

d *What would you say are the most important parts of Jewish worship? Why?*

e *'The most important thing is how you live your life not how and when you worship.' Do you agree? Give reasons to support different opinions.*

Topic 5: Religion in the faith community and the family

The Big Picture

In this Topic you will be exploring the key issues that affect Jewish religious and community life. You will understand:

- why the covenant is so important to Jews
- how and why Brit Milah, Bat Mitzvah, Bar Mitzvah and Kiddushin are celebrated
- why Jews believe kashrut to be important.

What?

You will:

- understand how and why the rites of passage are important to Jews
- understand what kashrut is and why it is important to Jews
- understand how kashrut and family life is used in Judaism as a source of belief and practice.

Why?

Because:

- it is important to understand the place of rites of passage and kashrut in religion and their influence on belief and practice
- many Jews see kashrut as fundamental to their identity and obedience to G-d.

How?

By:

- examining the origins and nature and the rites of passage and kashrut
- understanding the importance of the rites of passage and kashrut
- evaluating your own views about the role and importance of rites of passage, kashrut and family life to Jewish identity.

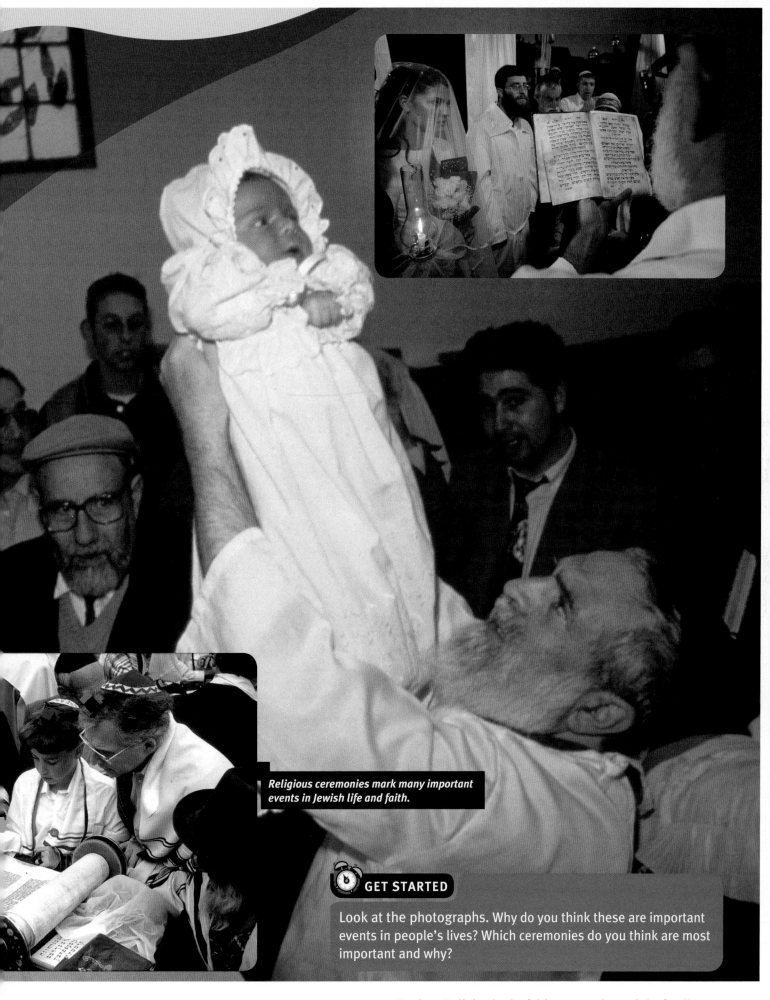

Religious ceremonies mark many important events in Jewish life and faith.

🕐 GET STARTED

Look at the photographs. Why do you think these are important events in people's lives? Which ceremonies do you think are most important and why?

Religion in the faith community and the family

KEY INFORMATION

- Many of the world's great religions have ceremonies called rites of passage, which link to events like birth, maturity, marriage and death.

- A rite of passage may tell you about the history of the religion, including some of the main beliefs and teachings.

- Brit Milah is the key ceremony making the child a partaker of the covenant.

- Bar and Bat Mitzvah have become important as ceremonies that mark religious maturity.

- Kiddushin (marriage) is seen as a spiritual commitment by Jews.

- Funerals and grieving are governed by Jewish teaching.

- Kashrut laws relate to keeping a kosher home and lifestyle.

- 'Gemilut Hasadim' means 'kind actions' and is a very important aspect of Jewish life, including supporting charities in the world and within individual Jewish communities.

KEY QUESTIONS

KNOWLEDGE AND UNDERSTANDING

Why is Brit Milah so important to Jews?

What are Bar and Bat Mitzvah seeking to achieve?

What attitudes should a person celebrating their Bar or Bat Mitzvah have?

Why is marriage so important to Jews?

Why are funerals so important to Jews?

Why do some Jews observe food laws and others not?

ANALYSIS AND EVALUATION

How can performing rites of passage be important today?

Why do different groups of Jews have different views about kashrut food laws?

Why do all Jews not believe the same things about rites of passage and kashrut if they all use the same holy books like the Tenakh and the Talmud?

Bar Mitzvah A boy's coming of age at 13 years old, usually marked by a synagogue ceremony and family celebration.

Bat Chayil Daughter of valour. *daughter of valour.*

Bat Mitzvah A girl's coming of age at 12 years old. May be marked differently in different communities.

Brit Milah Circumcision. It is a sign of the relationship between G-d and humanity.

chazan or cantor Leader of reading, singing and chanting in the services of some synagogues.

covenant G-d's promise to help the people of Israel.

huppah Canopy used for a wedding ceremony, under which the bride and groom stand.

Kabbalah Jewish mysticism.

Kaddish Prayer publicly recited by mourners.

kashrut Means 'pure'. Laws relating to keeping a kosher home and lifestyle.

Kashrut - pure

Ketubah A Jewish document that defines rights and obligations within Jewish marriage.

Kiddushin A Hebrew word applied to marriage; it means 'holy'.

Kiddushin - Holy - marriage

kosher Foods permitted by Jewish dietary laws.

minyan Quorum of ten men, over Bar Mitzvah age, required for a service. Progressive communities may include women but do not always require a minyan.

mohel Person trained to perform Brit Milah.

rite of passage Ceremony to mark an important part of life such as birth or marriage.

Shema A Jewish prayer affirming belief in one G-d. It is found in the Torah.

Shiva Seven days of intense mourning following the burial of a close relation. During this period, all ordinary work is prohibited.

tallit Prayer shawl. Four-cornered garment with fringes.

Talmud Mishnah (first writing down of the Oral Tradition) and Gemara (commentary on the Mishnah included in the Talmud), collected together.

Talmud = oral law = Mishna + Gemara (commentary)

tefillin Small leather boxes containing passages from the Torah, strapped on the forehead and arm for morning prayers on weekdays.

Tenakh The collected 35 books of the Jewish Bible, comprising three sections: Torah, Nevi'im, and Ketuvim (Te;Na;Kh).

Torah Law or teaching. The five books of Moses in the Scriptures.

FOR INTEREST The covenant is an important principle for Jews, as they believe that G-d has made a special relationship with them, based on following his laws. The sign of this relationship is that males should have the ceremony of Brit Milah.

Jewish birth ceremonies

The next two pages will help you to:

- explain the importance of Brit Milah
- evaluate the importance of a rite of passage to welcome a new baby.

Many events such as Brit Milah are followed by a party.

What is a rite of passage?

Many religions believe that it is important to acknowledge the key points of life. They believe that it is necessary to have a ceremony to help people at moments of change such as the arrival of a new child or a marriage. These ceremonies are called rites of passage.

The importance of Brit Milah

Jewish people call circumcision Brit Milah, which means 'the covenant of circumcision'. It is a sign of the relationship between G-d and humanity.

The covenant or promise was made between G-d and Abraham, when Abraham was instructed to circumcise himself and all the male members of his family as a sign of his commitment to G-d. One of the prayers used at the ceremony shows how important it is, as it links back to that story.

Prayer from the Brit Milah Service

Praised be thou, O Lord our G-d, King of the Universe who has commanded us to bring him in to the covenant of our father Abraham.

AO1 skills **ACTIVITIES**

Working with a partner, create a mind map to show all the things that you think you would need to do to prepare for a new baby in a family. Share your list with the class and try to agree the five most important things you would need to do in this situation.

Practices of the Brit Milah

Brit Milah should take place on the 8th day after the mother has given birth. However, if the baby is sick, the ceremony is delayed until the child has recovered.

Many circumcisions take place in the home of the family to whom the baby boy has been born. A trained professional called a mohel will perform the circumcision. The mohel will first of all place the baby boy on a special chair. It is believed that each time there is a Brit Milah, the spirit of the prophet Elijah is present, so the chair is a sign of his presence.

The mohel then gives the child to the **sandek**, who will hold him in his lap while the operation is taking place. The sandek is normally one of the grandfathers of the baby or a person regarded by the husband and wife of especial importance.

The father will recite a special blessing for his new son and the mohel will announce (in Hebrew), the name of the child. The parents will have agreed the name before the event; this marks the formal naming of the boy.

The whole group present will also pray that the child will faithfully follow the laws of the Torah and be a good person. Wine is passed round and there is a party to celebrate the life of the new child.

All Jews will have their sons circumcised. When the Reform Movement first began, they questioned whether they should continue with the ceremony, as they believed it was the meaning of the ceremony (commitment to G-d) that was more important than the ceremony itself. However, they decided that it was an important marker for being a Jew and could not be discarded.

Welcoming a baby girl

Some Jews also have a formal naming ceremony for their daughters, though this takes place when the child is 30 days old. Traditionally the father of a Jewish baby girl would announce his daughter's name in the synagogue at the Shabbat service about a month after she was born. The girl and her mother may be present although this is not required. It is often the case that the name is given at the next available service.

FOR DEBATE

Do you think that there should be a special ceremony for a child? Does it matter if the child is born into a religious or non-religious family?

Brit Milah
— covenant of circumcision

AO2 skills **ACTIVITIES**

'What matters most isn't the outward Brit Milah, but the inward meaning of it.' What do you think? What might a Jew think? Give reasons for your answer, showing that you have thought about it from more than one point of view.

'Girls are not of equal importance in Judaism, as is shown by the way they are greeted into the faith on their birth.' How might a Jew react to this comment? What do you think? Give reasons for your answer, showing a diversity of views within Judaism as well as clearly stating your own conclusion.

Why is Bar Mitzvah so important to Jews?

AO1 skills ACTIVITIES

Working with a partner, complete this sentence: 'A person can be said to be mature when...' Try to give at least three things a person will need to be seen as mature, and then share these with the class.

A young boy is helped to carry the Sefer Torah at his Bar Mitzvah.

The meaning and importance of Bar Mitzvah

When you become an adult, you are considered responsible. For Jews, Bar Mitzvah and Bat Mitzvah are times to mark the point when boys and girls become full members of the religion, when they should be reflecting on their actions and accepting the consequences, not seeing their parents as ultimately responsible.

Bar Mitzvah means 'Son of the Commandment' and marks the point at which a boy becomes a fully recognised member of the Jewish community.

The Bar Mitzvah ceremony

In many communities, for weeks before the ceremony, the boy will practise wearing the tallit (the prayer shawl) and will have learnt to put on the tefillin (the two leather boxes placed on the head and the arm to signify devotion to G-d in prayer).

The ceremony takes place on the Shabbat following the boy's 13th birthday. (Some Sephardic Jews may wait until later, but this is unusual.) For weeks before, the boy has been learning Hebrew (if Hebrew is not his first language) and practising the piece of the Torah that he will read in the service. A rabbi will help him to do this, either individually or as part of a class. His parents and family may well help him prepare.

On the day of the ceremony, the first act of the Bar Mitzvah in the synagogue will be when the boy's father makes a declaration that his son is now responsible for his own actions.

The Torah scrolls are then removed from the Ark and taken to the bimah, the reading desk in the centre of the synagogue. Using a yad (a pointer, often with a pointing finger at its end), the boy will read the passage of the Torah set. After reading he might give a short talk explaining the importance of what he has read.

After the reading, he is taken to a special party to celebrate his Bar Mitzvah. Here he will give a **derasha**, a mini-sermon that allows him to give thanks to his parents and gives him the chance to re-affirm his faith. Commitments have to be taken on publicly – the promises of the covenants of Abraham and Moses must be made personal to be effective.

He is now considered a full member of the synagogue. He can become part of the minyan, the group of ten that is necessary to make a synagogue a functioning place of worship. (In Orthodox synagogues, only males read from the Torah or form part of a minyan, though in Reform synagogues, a minyan can be both male and female.)

Among other things the boy:

- can be called to read from the Torah in any synagogue service
- can own what he possesses as personal property
- is seen as being old enough to marry legally according to Jewish law (but he cannot do so until the legal age of the country in which he is resident, which is normally between 16 and 18)
- must follow the 613 laws found in the Torah, trying to make sure that they are put into practice in his life.

FOR DEBATE

Do the different legal ages when a person can do something (for example, 17 to learn to drive, 18 to vote in a general election) make any sense? Should there just be one age for becoming mature in the eyes of the law?

RESEARCH NOTE

Using the Internet, find out more about how Bar Mitzvah developed as a ceremony.

AO2 skills ACTIVITIES

Write a 'Guide to your Bar Mitzvah' aimed at explaining what happens at the ceremony and the importance of it to a Jewish boy approaching 13. Make sure you explain key Jewish terms and words he will need to know.

'Thirteen is the wrong age to take on such responsibility.' What do you think of this statement? What might an Orthodox and a Reform Jew say? Give reasons for your answers, showing that you have considered more than one point of view.

Bat Mitzvah

The next two pages will help you to:

- examine the importance of Bat Mitzvah to Jews
- explain the ceremony of Bat Mitzvah.

A young Jewish girl at her Bat Mitzvah.

The importance of Bat Mitzvah

Bat Mitzvah means 'daughter of the commandment'. This means that a girl becomes a responsible female, being accountable for her actions before G-d at this age. Many Jews believe that a girl automatically becomes mature, so no ceremony is necessary. The Talmud teaches that this is when she reaches her 12th birthday. Boys do not reach adulthood until they turn 13. The difference in age serves to highlight the different roles accorded to men and women in Judaism.

The Talmud recognises that girls grow up earlier physically as well as emotionally. They are considered to be able to handle the responsibility that comes with maturity from a younger age.

AO1 skills **ACTIVITIES**

'Boys and girls should receive fair treatment, not equal treatment in schools.' Can something be fair but not equal? Should all students be treated exactly the same, regardless of their sex? Discuss this with a partner and then share your view in a class discussion.

The Kabbalah teaches that a person's spiritual being has several levels of soul to develop. A new level of soul (called 'neshama') comes into awareness at Bar/Bat Mitzvah time. This is the time when someone's moral awareness and sensitivity fully develops, enabling them to take complete responsibility and accept the implications of their actions.

The ceremony of Bat Mitzvah

Reform Jews decided that girls should be treated equally to boys and so devised the Bat Mitzvah. It generally takes place when the girl is 12 but some families will wait until she is 13. She too might read from the Torah and, in some synagogues, she may even give a d'var Torah, a talk based on the passage she has recited.

Becoming a Bat Mitzvah will include learning about the home and a woman's duties there. A girl will also learn about how to keep Shabbat and the festivals. As a gift at her party to celebrate, she may be given a set of Shabbat candles of her own, so that in time she might have them when she marries, for use with her new family.

Among the Orthodox community, there is a ceremony called **Bat Chayil** (daughter of valour). It was only during the 19th century that it gradually became the practice for Jewish families to hold special feasts in their home to mark their daughters' 12th birthdays. This often takes place on a Sunday, rather than Shabbat. Orthodox Jews do not believe that it is appropriate for a woman to read from the Torah scrolls themselves so she may read a passage from a book or from other parts of the Tenakh. Some Orthodox communities have a family celebration rather than a synagogue service. Some will have a service but the actual ceremony takes place with only women present.

Some synagogues have introduced a Bat Mitzvah test, which girls can sit three times a year. Those who are successful receive a certificate that can be given in the synagogue or another appropriate place to show that she has spent time studying the Torah and thinking about her role within the Jewish community.

At the party, Jews may give a present appropriate to the religious ceremony or they may bring gifts such as jewellery, books, clothes or picture frames. Some Jews think is important to give a significant gift such as a donation to a Jewish charity or planting a tree in Israel. They may give the girl a piece of jewellery based on a Jewish symbol such as the Magen David. To encourage her to think about how Jewish women can be important, they might buy her a biography of a famous person such as the former prime minister of Israel, Golda Meir.

FOR DEBATE

'The idea that girls are more mature than boys at 12 is wrong.' What do you think of this statement?

Bat Chayil
Daughter of Valour.

AO2 skills ACTIVITIES

'Bat Mitzvah shows how unequal women are in Judaism.' What do you think of this statement? What might a Jew think? Give reasons for your answer, referring to parts of the service to illustrate your point.

'There is a difference between becoming mature and getting older.' What does this mean? Do you agree?

Why is Kiddushin so important to Jews?

The next two pages will help you to:

- explain the importance of Kiddushin to Jews
- identify the main features of a Jewish marriage ceremony
- reflect on what you have learnt and express your own views about marriage.

A Jewish marriage taking place outdoors.

What is Kiddushin?

Kiddushin (the marriage ceremony) is seen as very important in Judaism because the relationship between men and women is stressed in the Jewish Scriptures.

In the book of Genesis, it says:

> **Genesis 2:24**
> *Hence a man leaves his father and mother and clings to his wife, so that they become one flesh.*

On the 6th day of Creation G-d gave humans the instruction to 'Be fertile and increase'. Therefore Judaism stresses the importance of marriage and bringing up children.

AO1 skills ACTIVITIES

You have been asked to help plan a wedding for a friend. Working with a partner, you have two minutes to list as many tasks as you would have to organise for the day to be a success. Whose help would you need?

The Kiddushin ceremony

Today the Jewish wedding ceremony takes place in a synagogue although this was unusual in the past. It is called a Kiddushin. The word 'kiddushin' means 'holy', as Jews think that marriage is holy, given by G-d to humanity to help them live as they should.

Before the wedding begins, the legal and religious document called a Ketubah is signed in which the groom makes a number of promises to his wife about how she will be treated by him and shares his hopes for their life together. This is signed and witnessed by people who are not related to the couple or to each other. This document may then hang in a frame over the couple's bed, as a sign of the commitment that has been made.

Features of the ceremony

The bride processes slowly down the aisle of the synagogue and joins the groom and the bridesmaids under a canopy called a huppah. Two people will lead the service. The first is the rabbi who will lead the formal and legally binding parts of the ceremony. In an Orthodox synagogue, this will always be a man – in a Reform or Liberal one, it may be a woman. The chazan (a person employed to sing prayers in services in the synagogue) sings a welcome: 'Blessed be the one who comes in the name of the Lord.' He will also sing other blessings.

The bride and groom stand under the huppah facing the Ark where the Torah is kept. This is a symbol that they want their marriage to be one that follows the laws of G-d. The huppah itself represents the new home that the couple will make together as a result of their wedding. Across the huppah is often written a blessing in Hebrew for the bride and groom. The chazan blesses a glass of wine and the bride and groom take a sip each, a symbol of their sharing a new life together.

The groom then places a ring on the right-hand forefinger of his bride and says a blessing. He gives her a ring and says: 'Behold, you are consecrated to Me by means of this ring, according to the rituals of Moses and Israel.' He will also read the promises he has made in the Ketubah.

The chazan recites seven blessings over the couple. These remind the couple of how G-d created humans in his own image and calls all present in the ceremony to rejoice at the joy G-d has brought at this moment.

The bridegroom takes the wine glass from which his wife and he drank and wraps it in a cloth. Placing it on the floor, he stamps on the glass. This is thought to be a symbolic way of saying that marriages will always go through good times and bad times. It also is a reminder of the sad fact that the Jerusalem Temple was destroyed by the Romans and has never been rebuilt.

The couple are now husband and wife. A wedding reception then takes place. No marriages are allowed on Shabbat (effectively ruling out Fridays and Saturdays), so Sundays and Tuesdays have become the two most popular days of the week for the ceremony to take place.

Most Jewish people will try to marry other Jews. Sometimes in the past, there were arranged marriages between Jewish families.

FOR DEBATE

'Marriage is out of date.' What do you think and why?

ACTIVITIES

'Marriage ceremonies are a waste of time and money.' What do you think? What might a Jewish person say? Give reasons for your answer, showing that you have thought about it from more than one point of view.

Why are funeral rites important to Jews?

The next two pages will help you to:

- identify the main features of Jewish funeral rituals
- explore how funeral rites reflect Jewish beliefs
- consider your own views about different ways of coping with death.

Funeral rites and Jewish beliefs

If a person is in a position when they know that they are going to die, then they are encouraged to recite the Shema and ask G-d for forgiveness of their sins.

Orthodox Jews forbid the cremation of a dead body and insist on it being buried, as they believe that there will be a physical resurrection that will require a body.

Reform Jews are not so concerned by this and allow cremation, believing that G-d will give a new body and that the outer casing of a soul is not of eternal consequence to him.

What happens at a Jewish funeral?

When death happens, there are certain rituals and traditions that should be followed. A body must be washed and the eyes and the mouth of the dead person are closed by a close relative of the deceased, as a mark of respect.

A Jewish man is normally buried in the simple white clothes he wears at the time of Yom Kippur to stress the humility he should have before G-d. A Jewish woman is buried in a simple dress. A man will have his tallit wrapped around him, with the tassles cut off the end, as he no longer needs to remember to follow all the commandments of the Law that they signify.

The body is covered by a shroud and then placed in a coffin. It is taken (in larger Jewish communities) to a cemetery, Bet Hahayim (House of the Living) where a rabbi will lead people in prayers which praise G-d's justice and ask that he will accept the deceased into eternal life.

A Jewish body is carried to burial.

ACTIVITIES

'When you die, you rot' (Bertrand Russell). Do you agree with this statement? Explain clearly what you think in a written answer and then share this with a partner. What do you think happens at the point of death?

The congregation will make small tears in the clothes they are wearing, as a symbol of their grief at the passing of the person, a tradition dating back to biblical times. For example, David tore his clothes when he heard of the death of Saul and Jonathan (II Samuel 1:11).

The coffin is then taken in the direction of the grave, though the pallbearers stop seven times to remember the seven vain things mentioned in the book of Ecclesiastes. These are:

- working too hard
- believing that money will help you
- the injustice in the world
- a person denying themselves pleasure
- the fleeting nature of political power
- the fleeting nature of relationships
- the fact of death, which we have to face.

As the body is lowered into the ground, the male mourners recite Kaddish, which is a declaration of G-d's holiness.

The importance of grieving

Judaism encourages those who have lost their loved ones to grieve, and has a pattern to help them to do so. This begins with a time known as Shiva. This is the first 7 days after the death, a time to withdraw and weep. Jews often sit on low stools during this time.

Second comes Sheloshin, which lasts 30 days. Here, the family return to the work they do but will not go on any social engagements during this time out of respect for their loved one. It is a time to reflect. On the first anniversary of the death, a Jewish family lights a candle to recall the person who has died and gives thanks to G-d for them.

If it was not already in place before the first month after the burial, the gravestone with the person's name is normally put up; it is a tradition in Judaism that small stones are placed on the grave as a mark of respect. Jews may do this for a non-Jew who has shown kindness to them. In the film *Schindler's List*, survivors of the Holocaust place stones on the grave of Oscar Schindler, who as a Gentile arranged to save many hundreds of them from extermination. The tradition may have begun when they lived in the desert and passing people would add stones to ensure the body was covered up.

Jews believe that if a person has led a good life, G-d will reward them. The wicked will be judged. The details of the afterlife are to be left to G-d rather than to be thought about now.

AO2 skills **ACTIVITIES**

'Jewish grieving ceremonies do more harm than good.' What do you think of the statement? What might a Jew say? Give reasons for your answers showing that you have thought about it from more than one point of view.

Kashrut

The next two pages will help you to:

- examine the Jewish food laws
- explain how what people eat can strengthen their religious belief.

ACTIVITIES

Are there foods that you do not eat? Why? Is it due to taste or an allergy?

Jews follow food laws called kashrut. These are examples of foods they are permitted to eat.

What is kashrut?

Kashrut are the laws that tell Jews how to keep a kosher home and lifestyle. Food laws are very important to Jewish people. Orthodox Jews try to follow exactly the laws about what they can and cannot eat from the Torah. Some Reform Jews think that the laws were made for a particular time and place. The word 'kosher' means 'clean', 'pure' and 'fit'. Kosher food is food that is fit for Jewish people to eat. How do you find out if something is kosher?

The rules of kosher food

In the book of Leviticus, various rules are given. An animal is kosher if it has two marks: it has cloven hooves and it chews the cud (it digests its food through four stomachs). Animals like cows, sheep, goats and deer are fine. Pigs, rabbits and camels are not kosher. The way an animal is killed is very important too, as it has to be slaughtered by a schochet, a specially trained person, following all the Jewish laws.

Fish are kosher if they have fins and scales such as cod and trout. Shellfish and oysters are non-kosher. Whale meat, although from a mammal, is treated by the Torah as if it were fish and therefore is also not allowed. Birds such as chicken, duck and turkey are kosher but some others like birds of prey such as eagles and vultures are non-kosher.

All vegetables and fruit are kosher but they must be checked to make sure that small insects or bugs, which are not kosher, have not infected them. Thorough washing in salt water should make sure that vegetables and fruit are edible. Eggs and milk are kosher as long as they come from kosher animals, but all eggs must be checked for spots of blood, which would make them non-kosher.

One rule that Jews try to follow at home is not to have a meal that has both milk and meat in it. If they had meat for a meal, they could not have custard, which would have milk in it, until a few hours later. In a Jewish home, there are often two sinks and two sets of crockery and cutlery for the different types of food.

Food and beliefs

It is very important to Jews that they know their food is kosher. You can go into some branches of supermarkets like Sainsbury's and find specially marked kosher sections. Kosher food will normally have on it a mark of approval, which shows a rabbi has approved the item and said that it has been produced in a kosher way.

If a product is suspected of not being kashrut, it can have serious implications for businesses. A few years ago, there was a concern in Israel that *Coca-Cola* was made in a non-kosher way. The board of the company was so alarmed that it allowed a leading rabbi to visit one of the plants where the drink is made. It even let him see the recipe for the drink, which no one outside the company is normally allowed to see. *Coca-Cola* was declared to be kosher. A kosher certificate was then awarded.

Sometimes, to make sure that they can get kosher food, Jewish people have set up their own shops to sell it, such as kosher butchers.

In London's East End, a group of Jews set up a Kosher Luncheon Club to provide good food, specialising in cooking fish dishes. It has become popular not just with Jews but also with other people who live in the area.

The requirement to eat kosher food means that Jews cannot simply go to any restaurant or shop to buy food. It also means that they usually cannot eat at the homes of non-Jews. This reminds them of who they are and of the laws that G-d has placed on them, and so strengthens their faith and also their sense of community.

AO2 skills **ACTIVITIES**

Plan a three-course meal for a Jewish friend so that the laws of kashrut are met and they have a variety of things to eat.

'Kashrut food laws are outdated.' What would an Orthodox and a Reform Jew say? What do you think? Show detailed evidence of Jewish teaching.

How does religious belief affect what a Jew might wear?

The next two pages will help you to:

- examine the Jewish laws that apply to what is worn
- explain how clothes show Jewish belief.

What people wear can reveal a great deal about what they believe is important.

Jewish laws about clothes

Many television programmes have suggested that what a person wears has a powerful effect on the way they think about themselves. It may re-enforce both positive and negative images they have of themselves. Many Jews believe that what you wear can reveal what you think about yourself and your relationship with G-d and others.

ACTIVITIES

Why do people choose the clothes they do? Try to identify at least five reasons, which you should then share with a partner. Which are the best and which are the worst reasons?

The Torah forbids the wearing of any clothes that are made from a mixture of wool and linen. This reflects the concept of purity as meaning 'being one thing' – such as in G-d begin one G-d. Anything that is mixed does not show the true unity that it should in order to reflect the creator. Later Jewish teaching also developed other principles that needed to be followed, especially the idea of modesty – not drawing attention to oneself.

The major principle is that of **shatnez**. Shatnez is a law of forbidden mixtures.

> **Leviticus 19:19**
>
> *You shall observe My laws. You shall not let your cattle mate with a different kind; you shall not sow your field with two kinds of seed; you shall not put on cloth from a mixture of two kinds of material.*

This was also developed in the later teaching of Judaism with many Jewish thinkers trying to apply the teaching practically. Some Orthodox Jews have established a special religious court to grant a kashrut certificate to women's clothing stores that they believe match the idea of modesty. Lycra has become popular among some Jewish women in recent years. However, as the fabric stretches over the body, this is a problem. According to some rabbis, this has the effect of enhancing those parts that should be hidden, breaking the law of modesty (see Meah Shearim on page 97).

Jewish beliefs about clothes

Other Jews have been influenced by the eco-kosher movement, so they are concerned about the way animals may have been treated or killed in order to become material for clothing. If an animal has not been killed in a way that follows the kosher rules, then it should be rejected. It is not wrong to have some clothes made from by-products of food manufacture like leather, but they must be treated in a way that reflects the laws.

Similarly, Jews may not wish to have clothes that have not been fairly traded. Many Jews believe that buying clothes that are the product of child labour or poorly paid workers does not fit with the idea of kosher being linked to purity. Such actions are therefore sinful.

RESEARCH NOTE

Do an Internet search to try and find a Jewish clothing company that follows the laws of kashrut.

FOR DEBATE

'No animal should suffer to make clothes you or I wear.' What do you think? Give reasons for your answer, showing that you have thought about it from more than one point of view.

AO2 **skills ACTIVITIES**

'Clothes express who we are inside.' What might a Jewish person say about this? What do you think? Give reasons for your answer, showing that you have thought about it from more than one point of view.

What do Jews mean by eco-kosher?

What are acceptable objects to Jews?

The next two pages will help you to:

- examine the Jewish laws of kashrut that apply to objects
- show how particular objects can relate to Jewish beliefs about purity
- explain what your own belief can show.

A kosher butcher's shop in the historic Marais district of Paris, France.

The importance of purity

Cleaning is a very important principle of kashrut and there are items that can help a Jew maintain cleanliness.

The mikveh is a special type of bath used by Jews who wish to observe the laws of their religion. There are examples of them dating back to the 1st century CE. On the hill fortress of Masada in the Judean desert, archaeologists found an example that had been used as far back as the time of Herod the Great in the years just before the Common Era began.

AO1 skills ACTIVITIES

'Cleanliness is next to godliness' (John Wesley). What does this mean? Do you agree? Give reasons for your answer, writing down your responses and then sharing them with the class.

The mikveh is normally about 5 metres in length and up to 3 metres deep. People who are seen as ritually impure (such as women at the end of their periods or people about to go into a special time of prayer) will use this special bath to help them prepare so that they can be made physically pure. Jews believe that the physical and the spiritual inside of a person both need to be cleaned by G-d.

Jews believe that it is important to be made holy before G-d. Sexual intercourse is forbidden during the onset and immediate days that follow a woman's period, until she has bathed in the mikveh.

Other aspects of kashrut

Kashrut has been applied to items other than food or clothes. Consumable items of any type have to fit with the idea of purity. Increasingly, kashrut has been linked not just with religious purity connected with G-d, but also with a way of talking about the natural order of things. The eco-kosher movement has encouraged Jews to think about boycotting goods that are not environmentally friendly.

Other Jews have suggested that fair-trade goods – where workers and producers are paid a fair price – are kashrut, as they reflect the pure justice of G-d in action. The Talmud encouraged an improvement in air quality near a tannery, where leather was being processed. There is a need to make sure that any investments in shares or in a bank are being used in a pure way, where justice is being practised.

Beliefs about purity

Kashrut is an issue that should affect all areas of a Jewish person's life. As well as food, it is important that people follow the rules for a kosher kitchen. This will ideally require two sinks – one to wash up meat dishes and one to deal with milk ones. It is important that the two do not become mixed up, as such confusion will lead to the kashrut rules being broken.

The utensils must reflect the teachings of kashrut as well. The Torah requires that if any utensils have previously been the property of Gentiles then they must be purified, by being immersed in a mikveh. As the Torah and, later, Jewish rabbis mention, articles made from metal and glass need blessing. Items of plastic or wood do not need this treatment. Jews differ as to whether porcelain or china objects require this or not.

FOR DEBATE

What do you think makes clothes acceptable to buy or not? Should you boycott clothes that are made in a way that harms the environment or are the result of unfair trade such as cheap child labour?

RESEARCH NOTE

Using the Internet, find out more about items in the kitchen and how they can become kashrut.

AO2 skills ACTIVITIES

'Rules about what you can own are wrong. Religion should not interfere in this area.' What do you think? What might Jews say? Make sure that you think about this from more than one point of view.

'You are what you own.' What do you think this means? Do you agree? What might the items you own say about the sort of person you are?

What is the role of religious communities for Jews?

The next two pages will help you to:

- understand the role of Jewish communities
- explain why family and community are important to Judaism
- evaluate the relevance of Jewish ideas about family and community.

Giving presents is traditional on each night of Hanukkah.

Life in the Jewish religious community

Some people see belonging to religion as just another club like the Scouts or a football team. Most Jewish people would reject this way of looking at their identity, which to them is not just about their faith but links to their ethnicity. They were most likely born Jewish. Some people do convert to Judaism; often this is when they are about to marry a Jewish person.

The Jewish community has a number of different groups within it. There are secular Jews, who are not religious but acknowledge the importance of their background. There are Jews who trace their ancestors back to Spain and North Africa, while others come from Eastern Europe. Two of the largest groups are the Orthodox and Reform Jews.

AO1 skills ACTIVITIES

Make a list of all the different groups you belong to (for example, a family, a school, a team). Which did you choose, which have you no say in? Are some of them temporary? Which groups might you like to be part of in the future?

Orthodox Jews

Orthodox Jews want things to remain unchanged because keeping traditions, teachings and festivals shows that they are of timeless relevance and there is no need to change. They believe these things will always be right, as they have come from G-d, who is eternal. They believe that the teachings in the Torah are timeless and will always need to be applied today. They look forward to the coming of a Messiah who will bring the world to peace. They are often very enthusiastic about the existence of the State of Israel.

Reform Jews

Reform Jews believe that teachings were expressed and provided in the way that people needed them when they first received them. They believe that people can take unchanging principles but apply them in new ways. So, for example, it was necessary to keep kosher food in the days of the Torah, but with modern methods of storing and preserving food, people do not need to be quite so restrictive.

Reform Jews believe that it is the duty of every Jew to try to bring peace into the world, rather than wait for a Messiah figure that will bring a golden age.

Family life

One of the Ten Commandments is about the importance of respect to parents.

Another of the commandments says, 'You shall not commit adultery'. That means a married person should not have sex with someone who is not already their husband or wife so that the family unit will be safe and not undermined by selfish sex.

Jews believe that a family is an important part of society. The members of it should respect each other. It is the responsibility of the children to care for their parents when they become elderly.

Jews also see the family as an important place where religion can be passed on, introducing children to the important festivals, the ideas of kosher and other aspects of being a Jew.

It is the responsibility of the parents to make sure that their children are brought up properly and to help them develop a career. The Talmud advises, 'Teach your son a trade or you teach him to become a robber.'

Marriage is seen as very important, so it is only in exceptional circumstances that there can be a divorce. The couple should only pursue this course if they have no other options and can prove that the marriage has effectively died.

FOR DEBATE

'Religions should adapt themselves to changing circumstances.' What do you think? Give reasons for your answers. What would a Reform or an Orthodox Jew say to this idea?

Exodus 20:12

Honour your father and your mother, that you may long endure on the land that the LORD your G-d is assigning to you.

AO2 skills ACTIVITIES

'Families are the building block of any society.' What does this mean? Would a Jewish person agree? Give reasons for your answer, remembering to include evidence from Jewish sources to back up your point of view.

'The different types of Jews show that religion just divides people.' What do you think? What might a Reform or an Orthodox Jew think about this? Give reasons for your answers.

What is Jewish belief about charity?

The next two pages will help you to:

- explore why Jews believe they have a responsibility to help and care for others
- evaluate your own beliefs about charity.

Poverty is found all around the world. The Torah teaches that people need to be 'openhanded to the poor'.

AO2 skills ACTIVITIES

Look at the list of people below. Which of them are most in need of help from a charity? Put them in order of importance for help, with 1 being the most in need and 5 being the least:

1 a single mother of two children under 5 in Britain
2 a homeless person in Britain
3 an AIDS orphan in Africa
4 a victim of a flood in Bangladesh
5 a refugee from a civil war in South America.

Discuss with a partner and try to give reasons for the choices you have made. Then discuss your choices as a class.

Charity and concern

Charity is the giving of money or resources to those who are less fortunate. Jews believe that they have a responsibility to help others and this will include giving where they can.

Many Jews believe that they should give a tenth of all they earn to help the poor. This is known as **tzedaka**, which is a Hebrew word meaning 'righteousness'. This money is seen as belonging to the poor, so not to give is seen as robbery. Whatever your means, you should try to give to help others.

There are appropriate ways to give. The worst one is to just hand over money to a person without thinking about it. If money is lent, it should be as a long-term, interest-free loan: you should not profit from someone's misfortune. The Jewish thinker Maimonides said, 'The best way of giving is to help a person help themselves so that they may become self-supporting.'

RESEARCH NOTE

Find out about the work of Jewish Care and plan a presentation on the charity.

How do Jews give to charity?

Many Jews have in their homes small collection boxes called pushkes. They think it is important to give some money to charities such as Jewish Care, which looks after the elderly and the disabled.

'Gemilut Hasadim' means 'kind actions', which covers all kinds of charitable work. This might include charities like Jewish Care or organisations like Tzedek, which works right the way across the world to help Jews in need.

Charity and beliefs

In the Torah, Jews are told that they should allow areas on the edge of their fields to be left and fruit that had fallen from trees should not be touched, so that the poor can be fed. In the book of Ruth in the Tenakh, the title character gleans the side of a field so that her mother-in-law Naomi and she can get corn to help them make bread, as they are poor.

The Ten Commandments warn people against stealing or wanting things that are not theirs. In the book of Proverbs, it says:

> **Proverbs 23:4**
> *Do not toil to gain wealth; Have the sense to desist.*

In the book of Deuteronomy, there is an instruction to all Jews:

> **Deuteronomy 15:11**
> *For there will never cease to be needy ones in your land, which is why I command you: open your hand to the poor and needy kinsman in your land.*

The Talmud also says that being poor is a miserable fate and that people should be helped to escape its problems. In another place it says, 'Poverty is worse than fifty plagues.' It also teaches, 'A poor man is reckoned as dead' – a way of showing that the quality of life for the poor can often be low.

The giving of charity will also help to protect Jews from developing a love of money, which will lead to an unhealthy obsession with possessions. As it says in the book of Ecclesiastes:

> **Ecclesiastes 5:10**
> *As his substance increases, so do those who consume it; what, then, does the success of its owner amount to but feasting his eyes?*

FOR DEBATE

There is an old saying: 'Give a man a fish, he will eat for a day. Teach him to fish, he will eat for a lifetime.' What does this mean? How might this apply to the Jewish person's attitude to charity?

AO2 skills **ACTIVITIES**

'People too easily run to charities for help.' What do you think about this? What might a Jew think? Give reasons for your answers, showing that you have thought about it from more than one point of view.

'Jews should concentrate on the next life, not worry about improving people's lives now.' What do you think an Orthodox and a Reform Jew might think? What do you think? Give reasons for your answers, showing that you have thought about it from more than one point of view.

Welcome to the Grade Studio

This Topic is about how the lives of Jews are affected by their faith. The most common problem with responses to questions on these topics is that they do not refer sufficiently to Judaism. It is not that these responses are wrong, but to get to the highest levels you need to show you have plenty of knowledge and understanding of the Jewish teachings and attitudes that lie behind the activities of Jewish individuals and communities, which you can apply as required.

Graded examples for this topic

AO1

AO1 questions test what you know and how well you can explain and analyse things. Let's look at an AO1 question to see what examiners expect you to do.

Question

Explain why kosher food laws are important to Jews.   [6 marks]

Student's answer

Kosher food laws are important because it is what G-d wants.

Examiner's comment

This answer is a start at answering the question, but the information is very weak. The explanation only refers to the fact that Jews believe this is what G-d wants. There is no real explanation given, so this would only receive the minimum marks (Level 1).

Student's answer

Kosher food laws are important because it is what G-d requires of the Jews in the Scriptures. In this way Jews know what they can and cannot eat and can live according to G-d's wishes.

Examiner's comment

The answer gives a slightly better account of the importance of keeping the food laws. However, it needs to use more examples. This is a reasonable response at Level 2, but needs more development.

Student's improved answer

Kosher food laws are important because it is what G-d requires of the Jews in the Scriptures. In this way Jews know what they can and cannot eat and can live according to G-d's wishes. The food laws are part of the 613 mitzvot. Keeping the food laws means that Jews often have to go to special shops to buy their food. They can only eat in kosher restaurants and they have to keep their kitchens at home kosher with different crockery, cutlery and pots and pans for meat and dairy products. In all these ways Jews come to feel close to G-d and also to other Jews.

Examiner's comment

This is an excellent answer, which clearly explains the importance of the food laws for a Jew (Level 3).

AO2 questions are about examining points of view and expressing your own views, using evidence and argument to support them. AO2 questions are worth 12 marks.

Examiners will use levels of response to judge the quality of your work and the best responses will have plenty of evidence to support different points of view. For AO2 there are four levels of response and for the top level the response will have a personal view supported by evidence and argument.

Question

'Worshipping G-d is important: what you eat is not.' Discuss this statement. You should include different, supported points of view and a personal viewpoint. You must refer to Judaism in your answer. **[12 marks]**

Student's answer	Examiner's comment
For Jews it is very important that they worship G-d regularly but it is also important that they follow all the food laws that G-d has told them to follow, as both these instructions are in the Torah. However, I think that it is obviously more important to worship G-d than to worry about what you eat.	This is a much better response. The answer gives a clear explanation of a possible Jewish view. However, it only gives one view and a personal opinion and so can only reach the top of Level 2.

Student's improved answer	Examiner's comment
For Jews it is very important that they worship G-d regularly but it is also important that they follow all the food laws that G-d has told them to follow, as both these instructions are in the Torah. Some Jews might say that times have changed since the food laws were given. Although it will always be important for Jews to worship G-d, they may feel that the food laws can be adjusted more to the 21st century and do not need to be so strictly observed now. However, I think that it is obviously more important to worship G-d than to worry about what you eat.	This is a very good answer. It gives clear explanations of two possible Jewish views as well as a personal opinion. This reaches Level 4.

These specimen answers provide an outline of how you could construct your response. Space does not allow us to give a full response. The examiner will be looking for more detail in your actual exam responses.

Remember and Reflect

AO1 Describe, explain and analyse, using knowledge and understanding

Find the answer on:

1 Explain, in one sentence, what each of the following key words means:
   a Brit Milah
   b sandek
   c mohel

PAGE 110, 111

2 Why is a Brit Milah so important to Jews?

PAGE 110, 111

3 Explain what Jews mean by the covenant.

PAGE 110

4 Explain why Bar and Bat Mitzvahs are important to Jews.

PAGE 112, 115

5 Why do Jews believe marriage (Kiddushin) is important?

PAGE 116, 117

6 Explain the different roles of the rabbi and the chazan in a Jewish marriage ceremony.

PAGE 117

7 Explain, giving examples, the important symbols or symbolic actions in a Jewish marriage ceremony.

PAGE 117

8 Explain, in one sentence, what each of the following words means:
   a Shiva
   b kashrut

PAGE 119, 120

9 Outline three ways in which kashrut food laws affect Jewish people.

PAGE 120, 121

10 Outline three ways in which being a Jew shapes a person's family life.

PAGE 126, 127

AO2 Use evidence and reasoned argument to express and evaluate personal responses, informed insights, and differing viewpoints

1   Answer these questions giving as much detail as possible. You should give at least three reasons to support your response. You should also show that you have taken account of opposite opinions.

a   *Jews find following kashrut food laws difficult. Do you think kashrut food laws are relevant in today's world? Do you believe kashrut laws are set by G-d? Why or why not? Compare your response with that of an Orthodox Jew, a Reform Jew and an atheist.*

b   *'Much of Judaism is irrelevant to the modern world.' How would an Orthodox Jew and a Reform Jew answer this? Refer to Jewish teaching and practice. What do you think? Give reasons for your answers, showing that you have thought about it from more than one point of view.*

c   *What problems might Jews face trying to live out their beliefs in Western culture?*

Topic 6: Sacred writings

The Big Picture

In this Topic you will:

- consider the importance of the Tenakh (Torah, Nevi'im and Ketuvim) in Jewish belief
- consider the importance of the Talmud for Jews
- consider the use of the Tenakh and Talmud in public and private worship
- express views about the importance of sacred writings and the respect that Jews show towards them.

What?

You will:

- develop your knowledge and understanding of key Jewish beliefs about the Tenakh and Talmud and their importance
- explain what these beliefs and ideas about the Tenakh and Talmud mean to Jews
- make links between these beliefs and ideas and what you think/believe.

Why?

Because:

- these beliefs and ideas about the Tenakh and Talmud underpin and are reflected in the ways Jews live their lives, for example, in helping them to decide what principles they live their lives by
- understanding people's beliefs can help you understand why they think and act the way they do
- understanding these beliefs helps you compare and contrast what others believe, and helps you think about your own beliefs and ideas.

How?

By:

- recalling and selecting information about Jewish beliefs and ideas about the Tenakh and the Talmud explaining their importance for people today
- thinking about the relevance of these beliefs in 21st-century Britain
- evaluating your own views about these beliefs.

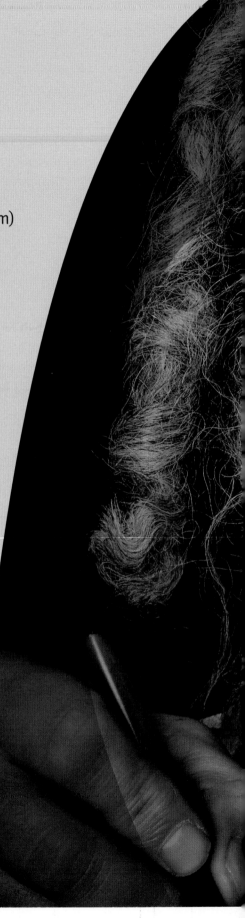

Torah study has always been an essential part of Jewish life.

'The Torah is irrelevant to the world today.' Do you agree or disagree? Give reasons. Do a survey to find out what people think about this question and why.

Develop your knowledge

Sacred writings

- Many of the world's great religions have a book, or books, which they consider to be sacred writings.

- Sacred books may contain the history of the religion, including the life of the founder and other key figures, and the main beliefs and teachings about how people should live. In Judaism, the sacred books are the Tenakh and Talmud.

- The Tenakh contains different kinds of literature including history, laws, prophecy, poetry and wisdom literature.

- The Tenakh is made up of 35 books and is divided into three parts.

  1 The first part is the Torah, which is made up of five books that Jews believe were written by Moses.

  2 The second part of the Tenakh is the Nevi'im (Prophets), which contains 19 books.

  3 The third part of the Tenakh is the Ketuvim (Writings), which contains 11 books.

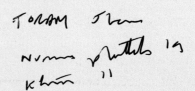

- The Talmud is also known as the Oral Torah and contains the Mishnah and Gemara.

- The sacred books are important to Jews because they are the source of Jewish beliefs; they are a guide to life and contain the word of G-d.

- Many Jews believe that the Scriptures are the inspired word of G-d and are literally true.

- The Jewish Scriptures (the Tenakh and Talmud) are used by Jews in their public and private worship and shown great respect.

KEY QUESTIONS

KNOWLEDGE AND UNDERSTANDING
How were the Jewish Scriptures compiled?

What do they contain?

Why are they important to Jews?

How do Jews use the Scriptures?

ANALYSIS AND EVALUATION
How can a collection of books written over 2000 years ago be important today?

What do Jews mean when they say the Scriptures are the word of G-d?

How can some of the things in the Scriptures be true when they contradict science?

Why do different groups of Jews treat the Scriptures differently?

Why do all Jews not believe the same things if they all use the same books?

Aramaic The original language of large sections of the books of Daniel and Ezra, and the main language of the Talmud.

Aron Hakodesh The focal point of the synagogue, containing Torah scrolls.

covenant G-d's promise to help the people of Israel.

Gemara Commentary on the Mishnah included in the Talmud.

Haftarah Passages from Nevi'im (Prophets) read in the synagogue (linked to weekly Torah and festival readings).

Ketuvim Writings. Third section of the Tenakh.

Midrash Collections of various Rabbinic commentaries on the Tenakh.

Mishnah First writing down of the Oral Tradition. An authoritative document forming part of the Talmud, codified around 200 CE.

mitzvot Commandment. The Torah contains 613 mitzvot.

Nevi'im Prophets. Second section of the Tenakh.

Sefer Torah Torah scroll. The five books of Moses handwritten on parchment and rolled to form a scroll.

Siddur Order. Daily prayer book.

Simchat Torah Rejoicing of the Law. Festival celebrating the completion and recommencement of the cycle of the weekly Torah reading.

Talmud Mishnah and Gemara, collected together.

Tenakh The collected books of the Jewish Bible, comprising three sections: Torah, Nevi'im, and Ketuvim (Te;Na;Kh).

Torah Law or teaching. The five books of Moses in the Scriptures.

yad Hand-held pointer used in reading the Sefer Torah.

FOR INTEREST 'Septuagint' is the name that is used for the ancient Greek translation of the Hebrew Tenakh. The term comes from the Latin word 'septuaginta' (seventy). This is because legend says that the High Priest of the Jerusalem Temple employed 70 translators for this work at the request of the Egyptian Emperor Ptolemy II. The books of the Torah were translated first, probably by the 3rd century BCE. They were used by Greek-speaking Jews who lived outside Palestine and could no longer understand Hebrew.

The nature of the Jewish Scriptures

The next two pages will help you to:

- identify the elements that make a book sacred
- examine how sacred books are seen by believers
- debate whether the idea of sacred is still relevant in a secular age.

Sikhs treat the Guru Granth Sahib Ji as though it was a human guru.

AO1 skills **ACTIVITIES**

Write a list of books that you think are particularly important. Why do you think that these books are important? Are they important just to you or are some of them important to many people? Compare your list with a partner's list.

What makes a book sacred?

'Sacred', like 'holy', means 'coming from G-d' and carries the authority of the divine.

Books may be believed to be sacred or holy to followers of a religion. Many religions have books or texts that they believe are sacred. In particular, there is the Bible for Christians, the Qur'an for Muslims and the Guru Granth Sahib Ji for Sikhs.

Some of the books, such as the Guru Granth Sahib Ji, are important because they were written by the founders of the faith. Others are believed to be the actual word of God. The Qur'an, in particular, was dictated to Muhammad by the Angel Jibril, direct from Allah.

The Jewish Scriptures consist of the Tenakh and the Talmud. Judaism teaches that the five books of the Torah, the first part of the Tenakh, are the exact words of G-d, given to Moses who wrote them down.

Although many books are very famous they are not sacred.

Some texts are also seen as sacred because of what they contain. The Acts of the Apostles and the letters in the Christian New Testament contain the teachings and life of the first years of Christianity.

> **Deuteronomy 31:24–26**
> *When Moses had put down in writing the words of this Teaching to the very end, Moses charged the Levites who carried the Ark of the Covenant of the Lord, saying: Take this book of Teaching and place it beside the Ark of the Covenant of the Lord your G-d, and let it remain there as a witness against you.*

Some believers regard a particular book as sacred as they believe that it is inspired by G-d. They may use the term 'the word of G-d' for their Scriptures as they believe that G-d has revealed the content of the book to the people who were responsible for writing it.

Some Jews believe that parts of the Jewish Scriptures are the words of humans trying to understand G-d.

Is the idea of sacred still relevant in a secular age?

There are many different religions in the world and many of them have sacred texts or writings. Most religions would say that their own sacred texts are the ones that everyone should follow, as they are the words of god. Some people might say that all these books cannot be the 'one' set of Scriptures that contain the actual words of god.

People who do not believe in any religion may find it difficult to understand why people should put such importance on a particular book. Some non-believers, however, may say that many of the teachings found in the Scriptures of the world's religions contain very important teachings about how people should treat each other.

 **ACTIVITIES**

'Only one book can be really sacred.' What do you think? How might a Jew respond to this? Give reasons for your answers, showing that you have thought about it from more than one point of view.

The importance of the Tenakh to Jews

The next two pages will help you to:

- explain why the Tenakh is important to Jews
- understand what the Tenakh contains
- consider the importance of the Tenakh for Jews.

Why is the Tenakh important for Jews and what does it contain?

The Jewish Scriptures are regarded as the word of G-d and so influence every aspect of Jewish life. The Jewish Scriptures are called the Tenakh in Hebrew.

The Tenakh is in three sections: Torah (Law (literally 'instruction' or 'direction')), Nevi'im (Prophets), Ketuvim (Writings). However, sometimes the whole of the Scriptures are referred to as the Torah. These three sections together make the Scriptures.

The initial letters of the three sections (T, N and K) make up the word TeNaKh. The Tenakh is written mainly in Hebrew with some sections in Aramaic.

An open Sefer Torah.

Torah

The Torah contains five books – Genesis, Exodus, Leviticus, Numbers and Deuteronomy. 'Torah' is Hebrew for 'law' or 'teaching'. The Torah is the most important part of the Scriptures because it contains the words that G-d spoke to Moses on Mount Sinai. The books of the Torah teach how people can live according to G-d's will.

The five books describe the creation of the world, the first 2000 years of history, the origin of the Jews, the period of slavery in Egypt, the Exodus, the giving of the Torah at Mount Sinai and some of the 613 mitzvot that Jews try to follow.

The Torah was received by Moses from G-d. Therefore the teachings of the Torah cannot develop or change. Anything that adds to the Torah is not a new revelation but just a commentary on what is already there.

Nevi'im

The books that form the Nevi'im are about the history of Israel, the conquest of the land of Canaan, and the work and teachings of the prophets.

The books are divided into two groups:

- Joshua, Judges, Samuel (parts 1 and 2), Kings (parts 1 and 2), Isaiah, Jeremiah, Ezekiel
- the 12 minor prophets: Hosea, Joel, Amos, Obadiah, Jonah, Micah, Nahum, Habbakuk, Zephaniah, Haggai, Zechariah, Malachi.

AO2 skills ACTIVITIES

'The Jewish Scriptures are so old that people cannot be expected to take the teachings in them literally.' How might a Jew react to this? What do you think? Give reasons for your answers.

Another example is found in relation to the slaughter of animals for food (see Deuteronomy 12:21).

Although this tells the Jews to slaughter cattle 'as I have commanded you', there are no instructions given – these instructions are again found in the Oral Torah.

Mishnah

Rabbi Yehudah Hanasi (Rabbi Judah the Prince) lived at a time when the Romans were persecuting the Jews around 200 CE. Until this time the Oral Torah had been passed on from teacher to teacher by word of mouth. With the Roman persecution, and emigration from Israel, people began to fear that it might be forgotten. Therefore Rabbi Yehudah wrote down the outline of the Oral Torah in the Mishnah.

The Mishnah has 63 parts (Mesechtos). Each of these gives the background for each topic of Jewish Law found in the Oral Torah.

The 63 sections are divided into six orders:

- Zeraim (seeds): agricultural laws, prayers and crops
- Moed (festivals): the laws for the Sabbath and festivals
- Nashim (women): betrothal, marriage and family law
- Nezikin (damages): civil and criminal law
- Kedoshim (holy matters): the Temple and sacrifices
- Taharos (purities): the laws of ritual purity.

The Mishnah also contains Halakhah, teachings on issues of Law, and Haggadah, guidance on preaching.

Gemara

Following the writing of the Mishnah, the persecutions continued and the rabbis of Babylon (Iraq) believed that there needed to be a more detailed version of the Oral Law. This is now called the **Gemara**. The rabbis of Israel worked on a similar version of the Law but were stopped by the persecutions.

Together the Mishnah and the Gemara form the Talmud (teachings). One of the most important commentators was Maimonides (1135–1204), Rabbi Moses ben Maimon. He wrote the Mishnah Torah, which was a 14-part classification of the teachings of the Talmud.

Midrash

The third of the Jewish books of the Oral Law is the Midrash (a collection of Rabbinic commentaries and interpretations of the Scriptures). This is the oldest collection of Jewish stories and legends and dates from around 200 CE.

> **Deuteronomy 12:21**
>
> *If the place that HASHEM, your G-d, will choose to place His Name [the Temple] will be far from you, you may slaughter from your cattle and your flocks that HASHEM has given you, as I have commanded you, and you may eat in your cities according to your heart's entire desire.*

AO2 skills **ACTIVITIES**

'Laws made up by humans can never be as important as ones that come from G-d.' How far do you agree with the comment? Give reasons for your answer and make sure that you give Jewish responses as well.

Moses Maimonides (1135–1204).

How are the Tenakh and Talmud used by Jews in public worship?

The next two pages will help you to:

- explain how the Tenakh and Talmud are used in public worship
- evaluate the importance of the Tenakh and Talmud for public worship.

AO1 skills **ACTIVITIES**

Using a copy of the Jewish Scriptures, find the following: Exodus 20:1; Isaiah 7:14; Ruth 1:1; Psalm 23:1; Micah 4:3.

How can you find a reference in the Tenakh?

Each book of the Tenakh has been divided into chapters and then smaller pieces of text known as verses. This is usually written like this: Genesis 1:1: this means the first verse of the first chapter of the book of Genesis, the first verse in the Torah.

The Tenakh and Talmud in public worship

Readings from the Torah are an essential part of worship in the synagogue. The Torah contains the Ten Commandments given to Moses on Mount Sinai, but also the 613 mitzvot (commandments), which show Jews how they should live.

Judaism teaches that if all the mitzvot are obeyed Jews will be cared for by G-d. If the commandments are ignored then Jews may suffer. In daily worship and readings from the Torah, the scrolls and the respect shown to them are an important part of worship.

There are places in the Torah where the text is unclear and difficult to understand, but tradition has provided an explanation of these. Where there are difficulties in interpreting the text, the Talmud or Oral Torah is used. Jews believe that the Oral Torah was given to Moses at the same time as G-d gave him the Written Torah and that it is intended to be used to interpret the written text.

When a piece of text simply cannot be understood but would make sense of one word was corrected, a rule called keri (read) and k'tiv (written) is used. The 'correct' word is read instead of the one that is actually written.

Torah scrolls being carried through the streets on the festival of Simchat Torah.

Torah readings in the synagogue

There are readings from the Torah in the synagogue on every Shabbat, on festivals, New Moons, fast days and every Monday and Thursday. Readings take place at the end of morning worship and during the afternoon service.

The lectionary (pattern of readings) is organised so that the whole of the Torah is read during the course of the year, beginning and ending on Simchat Torah, which is a festival that follows Sukkot. On Simchat Torah (Rejoicing in the Torah) the final words of the book of Deuteronomy, which detail the death of Moses, are read followed immediately by the first words of the book of Genesis so that the cycle starts again.

> **Deuteronomy 34:10–12**
>
> *Never again has there arisen in Israel a prophet like Moses, whom HASHEM had known face to face, as evidenced by all the signs and wonders that HASHEM sent him to perform in the land of Egypt, against Pharaoh and all his courtiers and all his land, and by all the strong hand and awesome power that Moses performed before the eyes of all Israel.*

> **Genesis 1:1–5**
>
> *In the beginning of G-d's creating the heavens and the earth – when the earth was astonishingly empty, with darkness upon the surface of the deep, and the Divine Presence hovered upon the surface of the waters – G-d said, 'Let there be light,' and there was light. G-d saw that the light was good, and G-d separated between the light and the darkness. G-d called to the light: 'Day,' and to the darkness He called: 'Night.' And there was evening and there was morning, one day.*

After the Torah reading a passage from the Nevi'im is read. This is chosen to link with the passage of the Torah that has been read. This other reading is called the Haftarah.

So, on Shabbat Vayeshev the Torah reading is Genesis 37:1–40:23 and the Haftarah is Amos 2:6–3:8. The Torah reading is the story of Joseph and his brothers up until the time that Joseph is put into prison in Egypt. In the Haftarah Amos is prophesying punishments on the tribes of Israel who were the descendants of Joseph's brothers.

Throughout the service, there are passages of prayers from the Siddur (daily prayer book). The Siddur contains passages from the Tenakh and the Talmud, which are used as prayers.

> **From the Amidah**
>
> *Forgive us, our Father, for we have erred; pardon us, our King, for we have wilfully sinned; for You pardon and forgive. Blessed are You, HASHEM, the gracious One Who pardons abundantly.*

ACTIVITIES

'The Torah is the most important part of Jewish worship.' What do you think? Give reasons, using evidence from this Topic and your own knowledge to justify your answer. What problems might a Jewish community find in using the Scriptures today?

How are the Tenakh and Talmud used by Jews in private worship?

Private worship

Private worship usually takes place in the home. Male Jews are required to pray three times a day and this is usually done in the home.

There are three daily periods of prayer:

- early morning: shacharit
- afternoon: mincha
- evening: ma-ariv.

All Jewish prayers are said facing east, towards Jerusalem. Each of the periods of prayer has Torah readings and prayers praising G-d. Jews may also pray spontaneously at any time when they feel that they want to speak to G-d.

During these times of prayer there are not only readings from the Torah but also passages from the Talmud:

The next two pages will help you to:

- explain how the Tenakh and Talmud are used in private worship
- evaluate the importance of the Tenakh and Talmud for private worship.

A Jewish man at prayer on Lag B'Omer.

Pikei Avot, Sayings of the Fathers, 1:1

Moses received the Torah from Sinai and transmitted it to Joshua; Joshua to the Elders; the Elders to the Prophets; and the Prophets transmitted it to the Men of the Great Assembly. They [the Men of the Great Assembly] said three things: Be deliberate in judgment; develop many disciples; and make a fence for the Torah.

Although most Jews would not keep a copy of the Sefer Torah at home, every Jewish family would have a copy of the Siddur (prayer book) and probably also a **Chumash** at home. The Chumash is a copy of the Torah that shows the passage for each day that it is to be read, together with the Haftarah (see page 147) for Sabbaths and festivals.

 **ACTIVITIES**

Working with a partner make a list of what influences what you do at home. Explain how you make decisions about what you do. Are the reasons for these decisions based on what your family say, or are they influenced by religion in any way?

Jews will study the Tenakh at home individually as well as use it to teach their children and to discuss the text with each other. In addition to prayer and reading from the Tenakh many Jews also study the Talmud at home. Continuing to learn more about their religion and passing it on to their children has always been a very important aspect of Judaism.

Deuteronomy 6:4–7

Hear, O Israel: HASHEM is our G-d, HASHEM is the One and Only. You shall love HASHEM, your G-d, with all your heart, with all your soul, and with all your resources. And these matters that I command you today shall be upon your heart. You shall teach them thoroughly to your children and you shall speak of them while you sit in your home, while you walk on the way, when you retire and when you arise.

As well as texts to be studied at home, the Tenakh and the Talmud play a very important part in Jewish home life.

Passages from the Siddur are read before and after meals.

Grace after meals – first blessing

Blessed are You, HASHEM, our G-d, King of the universe, Who nourishes the entire world, in His goodness – with grace, with kindness, and with mercy. He gives nourishment to all flesh, for His kindness is eternal. And through His great goodness, we have never lacked, and may we never lack, nourishment, for all eternity. For the sake of His Great Name, because He is G-d Who nourishes and sustains all, and benefits all, and He prepares food for all of His creatures which He has created. Blessed are You, HASHEM, Who nourishes all. Amen.

Instructions for keeping a kosher home, for food and clothes, are also found in the Scriptures. Every time that Jews are following one of the 613 mitzvot, they are worshipping G-d.

An 18th-century miniature manuscript 'Grace Before Meals and Other Benedictions'.

AO2 skills ACTIVITIES

'For Jewish worship the Torah is more important than the Talmud.' Do you agree with this statement? Give reasons for your answer and include what a Jew might say in response.

How do Jews show respect to the Jewish Scriptures?

The next two pages will help you to:

- explain how Jews show respect to the Scriptures
- explore why Jews show such respect towards the Scriptures.

ACTIVITIES

Imagine that an important person is coming to visit your home. How might you prepare for their visit? How do these actions link to the idea about the respect the person is shown? Share your ideas with the rest of the class.

A yad is used so that people do not touch the text with their fingers.

Sefer Torah

The Torah scrolls used in the synagogue are called the Sefer Torah. This consists of the first five books of the Jewish Scriptures: Genesis, Exodus, Leviticus, Numbers and Deuteronomy.

The Torah is always treated with the greatest respect by all Jews. The text is handwritten on large sheets of animal skin and placed on long rollers. The scrolls are carefully copied by hand by a specially trained scribe using a turkey or goose feather.

Hebrew is written from right to left across the page. The Torah scrolls are often decorated with elaborate covers and have bells and other decorations hung on them. When they are not being used they are kept in a special cupboard in the synagogue called the Aron Hakodesh (the Ark).

When they are being read they are never touched by hand but a yad (pointer) is used so that the reader can follow the text.

The great respect shown to the Torah emphasises its importance to Jews as the Scripture that contains the truth about G-d and about the relationship between G-d and the Jews.

The Sefer Torah is dressed and decorated with care. The types of covering used vary between Ashkenazi and Sephardic Jews.

Ashkenazi scrolls

When Ashkenazi scrolls are rolled up, the rollers are brought together and tied with a linen binder. They are then wrapped in a mantle, which is an outer garment made from a rich material such as velvet. The mantle is open at the base to allow the scrolls to be placed inside. There are usually two holes at the top of the mantle to allow the tops of the staves or rollers (Etz Chaim – the Tree of Life) to come through.

A silver breastplate is then hung over the mantle, decorated with Jewish symbols such as pillars, crowns and flowers. This represents the breastplate worn by the High Priest in the Jerusalem Temple.

Ashkenazi scrolls.

On top of the staves are the rimmonim – clusters of silver bells that ring when the Torah is being carried.

Sephardi scrolls

The scrolls of Sephardi Jews are placed in a wooden or metal case, which is carved or engraved and richly decorated. The case is in two halves and hinged so that it can be opened like a book and the scroll displayed. The text is then read without the scroll being removed from its case. The correct place in the text can be found by turning the ends of the staves that protrude from the top of the case. This rotates the scroll.

Sefer Torah in the synagogue

When the Sefer Torah is not in use, it is kept in a special cupboard within the synagogue, known as the Ark. During worship the Sefer Torah is taken out of the Ark and is carried around for everyone to see.

As the scrolls are carried through the synagogue, the congregation stand and follow the procession, turning so that they are always facing the scrolls. Those who are near enough to reach let the tassels of their tallit touch the cover and then kiss the tassels as a mark of devotion.

Finally, the Torah reaches the bimah (reading desk), where the coverings are removed. The scroll is unrolled a little, and then held high above the head and rotated slowly so that everyone can see the writing.

Sefer Torah are always shown the greatest respect, even in old age. When a scroll has become damaged or too old to be used, it is not destroyed but, instead, placed in a **genizah**. This is a special storage room in a synagogue where old scrolls and ritual objects can be stored with respect when they are no longer fit to be used. Eventually these are buried in a cemetery.

AO2 skills **ACTIVITIES**

'The Jewish holy books are too old to have anything useful to say to modern people.' What do you think a Jew would say to this? What do you think? Give reasons for your answers, making sure that you use Jewish teaching and practice to illustrate your answer.

Are the Jewish Scriptures true?

Beliefs about truth and the Jewish Scriptures

What do we mean when we say that something is true? Scientific truth means that experiments can prove something is a matter of fact because they can be repeated with the same result.

If people say that the Jewish Scriptures are true, does it mean that they are factually accurate and can be checked? Many Jews would say that the Scriptures are true and contain fact but would not say that they can be checked and proven. Believers say that they are true because they believe that they are.

There are many stories in the Jewish Scriptures that may seem to contradict modern science. Miracles such as the control of natural events and the story of the Creation of the world can be seen as disagreeing with scientific theories. However, this does not mean that the Jewish Scriptures are not true.

The Scriptures were written in a time when the laws of science were unknown. Disease, death and natural disasters were often seen as punishments for sin. It would therefore be unrealistic to say that the Scriptures contained scientific truth.

In addition, many people spend a lot of their time watching television or reading books that are clearly fiction and untrue. However, although the actual stories may not be true in themselves, this does not mean that they do not include very important truths about life and how people behave.

The Jewish Scriptures and myth

In the past many people used stories to explain difficult ideas or things that they did not understand, such as earthquakes, the weather and death. Some people believe that parts of the Scriptures should be approached in this way.

These parts of the Scriptures can be described as myths: a probably fictitious story that contains an important teaching about history or a natural event.

ACTIVITIES

What do we read, which we think of as true? Discuss this question with a partner. Consider how people make judgements about whether something is true or not.

This means that, although a myth may not be literally true in the way in which news reports are expected to be, the ideas and teachings it contains may be true.

An example of a myth might be the story of the Flood in the book of Genesis. Many explorers have spent lifetimes looking for the wreck of Noah's Ark. Although it is possible that one day someone might find the wreck, it would not change the importance of the story in any way. The point of the story is to show that G-d could punish people but will always choose to save them.

Over the last 150 years many scholars have worked on the texts of the Scriptures. They have concluded that much of the information they contain is true, but often not true in the sense of being historically accurate concerning dates.

This does not mean that the Scriptures themselves are untrue in the sense of being false or a lie.

Do the Jewish Scriptures have a purpose in modern society?

Many Jews believe that the Jewish Scriptures are factually true, as they are the actual words of G-d.

Other Jews believe that a debate about the 'truth' of the Scriptures is a distraction from what is really important, and that the moral teaching comes through whether the stories are factually true or not. These Jews might say that, although the word of G-d may not be identical to the words of the Scriptures, the word of G-d nevertheless comes through the texts to believers as they read. Jews who take this view may believe that the Scriptures are inspiring and that G-d speaks to them, personally guiding their conduct, and gives them spiritual support regardless of whether every detail is factually true.

It is important to remember that Jews regard the five books of the Torah differently from the rest of the Tenakh. This still does not mean that some Jews regard them as literally, factually true, but that they do have a greater claim to being G-d's word.

ACTIVITIES

'If the Scriptures are made up, then they cannot be used to help us to live good lives now.' How might a Jew answer this? What do you think?

Welcome to the Grade Studio

In this Grade Studio we will look at the longer AO1 responses required for part (d) of the question, which is worth 6 marks. Part (d) of each question will be marked according to levels. For AO1, there are three levels. A good response to part (d) will be well organised, contain relevant knowledge and will have a full, well-developed explanation. If required, you should analyse the Topic, which means you might make a comparison between two aspects of the Topic.

Graded examples for this topic

AO1

AO1 questions test what you know and how well you can explain and analyse things. Let's look at an AO1 question to see what examiners expect you to do.

Question

Describe two kinds of literature in the Tenakh and explain why they might be important to Jews. **[6 marks]**

Student's answer

The Jewish Scriptures contain the Law and History. These are important because they show them how to live.

Examiner's comment

This is a start to responding to the question, but the answer is weak. The explanation only refers to the literature being important because it tells people what to do. There is no real explanation. This response is only Level 1.

Student's improved answer

The Jewish Scriptures contain Law and History as well as Prophecy, Poetry, Liturgy and Wisdom literature. Each of these are important because they help Jews to learn about their history and what happened to the first Jews. They can learn about the way in which the relationship between G-d and the Jews developed.

The Prophecy shows what G-d wants from people. However, it also shows what can happen if people disobey G-d.

The three groups of Poetry, Liturgy and Wisdom show the ways in which people who were writing the Scriptures tried to understand G-d and their relationship with G-d. This can also help Jews today to understand more about G-d and their religion.

Examiner's comment

This is an excellent answer. The candidate could have limited the answer to just some examples and perhaps explained them in more depth but this is another way of answering the question where all the types of literature in the Jewish Scriptures are considered.

AO2 questions are about examining points of view and expressing your own views, using evidence and argument to support them. AO2 questions are worth 12 marks.

Examiners will use levels of response to judge the quality of your work and the best responses will have plenty of evidence to support different points of view. For AO2 there are four levels of response and for the top level the response will have a personal view supported by evidence and argument.

Question

'The Torah is more important than the Talmud.' Discuss this statement. You should include different, supported points of view and a personal viewpoint. You must refer to Judaism in your answer. **[12 marks]**

Student's answer

The Torah was written by G-d and is his word, so it must be more important than the Talmud, which was written by humans.

I do not believe that either of them is important because I am not a Jew.

Examiner's comment

This is a better response. The answer gives an explanation of a possible Jewish view. However, it only gives one view and an undeveloped personal opinion and so can only reach Level 2.

Student's improved answer

Some people might say that the Torah was written by G-d and is his word, so it must be more important than the Talmud, which was written by humans. However, many Jews believe that Moses received the Written Torah and the Oral Torah from G-d on Mount Sinai and therefore they can be seen as equally important as they are both the word of G-d, just given in different ways. Also Jews need the Talmud in order to understand the Written Torah fully.

I do not believe that either of them is important because I am not a Jew. However, if I was Jewish I think that I would believe that the Torah was important because it is seen as the word of G-d.

Examiner's comment

This is a very good answer. It gives clear explanations of two possible Jewish views as well as a personal opinion. This reaches Level 4.

These specimen answers provide an outline of how you could construct your response. Space does not allow us to give a full response. The examiner will be looking for more detail in your actual exam responses.

Remember and Reflect

AO1 Describe, explain and analyse, using knowledge and understanding

Find the answer on:

1 Explain, in one sentence, what each of the following key words means:
   a Torah
   b Nevi'im
   c Tenakh

PAGE 137

2 Why is the Tenakh important to Jews?

PAGE 140

3 Explain what Jews may understand by the term 'the word of G-d'.

PAGE 153

4 Explain what Jews mean by the authority of the Torah.

PAGE 138

5 Why do Jews believe the Torah is so important?

PAGE 140

6 Explain, giving examples, the different types of books you will find in the Jewish Scriptures.

PAGE 140, 141

7 Explain, giving examples, what is found in the Pseudepigrapha.

PAGE 141

8 Explain, in one sentence, what each of the following words means:
   a prophecy
   b psalms
   c liturgy

PAGE 143

9 Outline how Jews use the Scriptures in public worship.

PAGE 146, 147

10 Outline how Jews use the Scriptures in private worship.

PAGE 148, 149

11 Write a sentence to explain the following:
   a yad
   b Sefer Torah
   c Aron Hakodesh

PAGE 150

AO2 Use evidence and reasoned argument to express and evaluate personal responses, informed insights, and differing viewpoints

1 Answer the following, giving as much detail as possible. You should give at least three reasons to support your response and also show that you have taken into account opposite opinions.

   a   *Jews must find it difficult to believe in the Scriptures as being literally true in the 21st century.*

   b   *Do you think Jewish teaching contained in the Scriptures is relevant in today's world?*

   c   *Do you believe the Torah is a holy book from G-d? Why or why not? Compare your response with that of a Jew and an atheist.*

   d   *What would you say are the essential things a Jew has to believe about the Torah? Why?*

2 'The Scriptures are a collection of books, not just one book.' How might this help Jews explain the importance of the Tenakh? What problems might be caused by the idea of the Tenakh being a library?

Exam**Café**

Welcome

Welcome to Exam Café. Here you can get ready for your exam through a range of revision tools and exam preparation activities designed to help you get the most out of your revision time.

Tools and Tips

Now you have finished the course/Topic, it is time to revise and prepare for the examination. A key to any exam is the revision and preparation leading up to it. The key to good revision is to 'work smart'. This section will guide you in knowing what is needed for success and, just as important, what is not. So don't panic! Think positive because the examiner will. GCSE is about what you *can* do, not what you can't.

Key points to note at this stage

1 Your revision will need to focus on what the examiner is looking for in the answers so that you can achieve the best possible mark. Remember that the examiners are looking for the AO1 and AO2 assessment objectives. Each of these objectives is worth 50 per cent of the total mark.

2 You also need to know that the exam questions on the paper are designed to test your performance with both AO1 and AO2 objectives. Each question will be made up of five parts:

- Four AO1 parts, of which three check your knowledge and one tests your understanding and analysis

- One question testing AO2 – your ability to consider different points of view on a particular issue and how much you can express your own points of view with relevant evidence and argument.

Once you understand what the examiner is looking for, it will be time to turn to your revision programme.

How to get started

An important key to success with any exam is the preparation beforehand. While few people enjoy the process of revision, it is something that is vital for success. Your class teacher will also discuss revision with you. Below are some suggestions and ideas that can be employed:

1 It is vital to revise in plenty of time before the exam. Do not leave everything to the last minute.

2 Design a revision timetable and be realistic about what can be achieved.

3 Revision is a personal matter and we all learn in different ways. Remember that many revision skills can be transferred between different subjects.

4 These are some suggested revision techniques:
  - Create summary cards for each topic – a maximum of 5–10 bullet points on each card.
  - Create lists of key words and terms. Ask somebody to test you on them or hang them around the house.
  - Create a mind map to summarise a major topic.
  - Design cards with a word or idea on one side and a question/ definition or answer on the other. These allow you to be tested by family members or friends who may not have much subject knowledge.
  - Create an A–Z list on a certain topic. This involves writing the 26 letters of the alphabet down the side of a page and then having to write a key word or teaching connected to that topic for each letter.
  - Remember that religious teachings do not have to be learned word-for-word. It is acceptable to paraphrase them.

5 Break your revision sessions of 5–10 minutes to start with (this can be increased as you become much better at it). Give yourself a short break (of about 5 minutes) and then go back to revising. Remember that spending time revising when nothing is going in is as bad as doing no revision at all.

6 Try answering questions on past papers then marking them with the mark scheme yourself. Alternatively, you can write your own questions and develop your own mark scheme. Answer the questions and use the levels of response to mark them.

7 Finally, remember that if you go into revision with a negative attitude you are ultimately going to make it much tougher on yourself.

Revision
Common errors and mistakes

So the day of the exam has arrived. Remember that you are not the first to sit exams and you will not be the last. However, learn from the experience of others and do not fall into any of the following exam traps:

Misreading the question: Take a minute and read the question carefully. Surprisingly, a large number of candidates do not read the questions properly. They simply see a word or miss a point and feel they have to start writing. No matter how good your answer is, if it does not answer the question it will not gain you any marks.

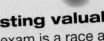

Wasting valuable time: The exam is a race against the clock. Match the length of your response to the number of marks being awarded. A one-mark question can be answered with a single word or a sentence and not a paragraph.

Poor selection of knowledge: Choose good examples that help you to develop and explain your ideas.

Disorganised waffle: Written answers, especially AO2 style answers, require you to plan your answer carefully. It requires a range of viewpoints including religious responses and your own views. Be careful and do not let your own views take over.

Know the exam paper: Make sure that you fully understand the layout and instructions for the exam paper. In particular, focus on which questions you must do and how many questions you are required to do.

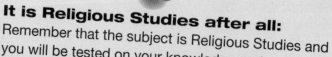

It is Religious Studies after all: Remember that the subject is Religious Studies and you will be tested on your knowledge and understanding of religion and its impact on the lives of individuals and communities. Make sure your answers contain relevant religious ideas.

Revision check list

The details of the course are known as the Specification. It is broken down into the Topics listed below. There is a summary of the key areas within each Topic that you need to know about.

TOPIC 1 CORE BELIEFS

For this Topic you must:
- know what Jews believe about the nature of G-d
- understand Jewish beliefs about the Messiah and the Messianic Age
- know and understand the meaning of 'covenant'
- understand the covenants with Abraham
- understand the covenant with Moses
- understand Jewish beliefs about the Law and the mitzvot
- be able to explain Jewish beliefs about life after death.

TOPIC 2 SPECIAL DAYS AND PILGRIMAGES

For this Topic you must:
- know and understand the importance for Jews of:
  - Shabbat
  - Rosh Hashanah
  - Yom Kippur
  - the pilgrim festivals, Pesach, Shavuot and Sukkot
- explain the role pilgrimage has played in the spiritual life of Judaism.

TOPIC 3 MAJOR DIVISIONS AND INTERPRETATIONS

For this Topic you must:
- know and understand the main similarities and differences between the following Jewish groups:
  - Hasidic
  - Orthodox
  - Reform
  - Liberal/Progressive
- be able to explain why there are different groups in Judaism and how these differences might affect the lifestyles and outlooks of Jews in the modern world
- be able to explain important issues in Judaism with reference to:
  - Zionism
  - The land and state of Israel
  - Twentieth Century Holocaust/Shoah.

TOPIC 4 PLACES AND FORMS OF WORSHIP

For this Topic you must:
- know and understand what Jewish places of worship might look like and what they show about Jewish beliefs
- know and understand the key features of Jewish places of worship, their meaning and purpose
- be able to explain the ways that Jews express their beliefs through different forms of worship.

ExamCafé

TOPIC 5 RELIGION IN THE FAITH COMMUNITY AND THE FAMILY

For this Topic you must:

- know and understand why the covenant is so important to Jews
- know how and why Brit Milah, Bat Mitzvah, Bar Mitzvah and Kiddushin are celebrated
- explain why Jews believe kashrut to be important.

TOPIC 6 SACRED WRITINGS

For this Topic you must:

- know and understand the importance of the Tenakh, the Torah, Nevi'im and Ketuvim, in Jewish belief
- know and understand the importance of the Talmud for Jews
- know and understand the use of the Tenakh and Talmud in public and private worship
- be able to express views about the importance of sacred writings and the respect that Jews show towards them.

Exam preparation
Sample student answers

Now you have done some serious revision it is time to see what sort of response to the questions will get good marks in the exam. Here are some examples of responses with comments from the examiner to show you what is good about them and how they could be improved.

Remember examiners will use levels of response for part d which is AO1 and part e which is AO2. For parts a, b and c responses will be point marked. This means that if there is one mark allocated for the question, only one point is expected, if two marks are allocated, then two points are expected and so on. Part a is worth one mark, b two marks and c three marks.

Here are some AO1 point-marked questions and example responses from Topic 6: Sacred writings.

What is a covenant? (1 mark)

A covenant is an agreement or promise between two people.

Examiner Tip

'What is?' just means describe something – in this case, covenant.

AO1 Part (d) questions

Some AO1 answers are marked in levels of response. These are part d of the questions and are worth six marks each. However, just because they are worth six marks, it does not mean that examiners want to see six short points or three developed points in the answer. Instead, the examiner is looking for a level of understanding. The higher the level then the higher the level of understanding required. This could be done by referring to several points and expanding each a little or by developing one or two points in greater detail. Below is a sample answer.

Examiner Tip
When answering this question, ask yourself the question 'Why?' as soon as you have written down a reason. There are different levels of explanation, and the examiner is looking for depth, not for a superficial level.

> **Explain what Jews believe about the covenant with Moses.** (6 marks)

Response 1

Jews believe that G-d made a covenant with Moses when the Israelites were in the desert and gave him the Ten Commandments. Jews are still required to follow the Ten Commandments today.

Examiner says
This is satisfactory response, reaching Level 2. The information given is relevant, and accurate reasons have been chosen. However, the response is not well developed and is essentially one-sided, giving only one explanation.

Response 2

Jews believe that G-d made a covenant with Moses on Mount Sinai when the Israelites were wandering in the desert for forty years. Part of this covenant was the Ten Commandments. Moses brought two tablets of stone down from the mountain with the Ten Commandments written on them. They were then placed in the Ark of the Covenant. The Commandments lay down laws about how the Jews should behave towards G-d and also towards other people. Jews are still required to follow the Ten Commandments today. They form part of the 613 mitzvot which are found in the Torah.

Examiner says
This is a good response. It contains much of the satisfactory response but it is much more developed. The reasons for different views are explained. This response would reach Level 3.

AO2

Part e of each question in the exam will involve an AO2 question asking you to explain different points of view about a particular issue. It also gives you an opportunity to present your own personal viewpoint. However, please remember that all viewpoints on a particular issue must be backed up with good evidence, argument and reasoning. Part e of each question is worth 12 marks, or 50 per cent of the total, so it is important to think carefully about how you are going to tackle these questions.

Planning an AO2 answer

These questions want different points of view about a particular issue. Your answer could therefore be structured in the following way:

Paragraph 1: Explain a view which will *agree* with the statement in the question. Offer evidence, beliefs and teachings to back up the point of view.

Paragraph 2: Explain a different view from what the statement is suggesting. Again, you need to offer evidence, beliefs and teachings to back up your point of view.

Paragraph 3: Include your own personal viewpoint about the issue raised. Again, you need to offer evidence, belief and arguments to support your point of view. The examiner does not mind which point of view you take, there is no right or wrong answer. Instead, the examiner is interested in your ability to reason and argue. If you really do not have a strong point of view on this issue just simply go for the viewpoint which you can best argue.

Here is an AO2 question and some example responses from Topic 2: Special days and pilgrimages.

> **'Jews should forget their differences and work together.'**   (12 marks)

Response 1

If all Jews are followers of G-d's teachings then there is no reason why they should not all work and worship together.

Examiner says

This is Level 1. There is only one view and it has little support to back it up. This is a simplistic response and shows limited understanding of the question. There is no use of technical terms.

Response 2

If all Jews are followers of G-d's teachings then there is no reason why they should not all work and worship together. In this way Judaism would be stronger and have more influence. Some Jews might feel that the differences between them are too important for them to be able to come together.

Response 3

If all Jews follow G-d's teachings then there is no reason why they should not all work and worship together. In this way Judaism would be stronger and have more influence. Some Jews from different groups do work together, particularly for charitable causes.

Some Jews might feel that the differences between them are too important for them to be able to come together. They may feel that they have different beliefs, for example about the authority of the Torah, or whether women can become rabbis and that these make it impossible for them to unite.

I think that if they really are all followers of G-d then they should unite.

Response 4

If all Jews follow G-d's teachings then there is no reason why they should not all work and worship together. In this way Judaism would be stronger and have more influence. Some Jews from different groups do work together, particularly for charitable causes.

They may feel that they have different beliefs, for example about the authority of the Torah, or whether women can become rabbis and that these make it impossible for them to unite.

I think that if they really are all followers of G-d's teachings then everyone should work as hard as possible to unite into one group for this must have been what G-d intende

ExamCafé

Understanding exam language

Examiners try to keep questions short and clear. To do this they use special trigger words to hint at how you should respond to the questions. Below is a list of common trigger words. You should familiarise yourself with these words:

State
Usually used in AO1 questions worth 1–3 marks. This means write down a fact about something. For example, *State the pilgrim festivals*.

Give
This is used instead of 'state' and requires the same sort of response.

List
This is used instead of 'give' or 'state' and requires the same sort of response.

Describe
This is used in AO1 questions and means 'tell the examiner factual information about the item or idea'. An example is, *Describe what happens at Pesach*, which means 'write down factual information about the celebration of Pesach'.

Give an account of
This is asking for the same sort of response as 'describe'. For example, *Give an account of Jewish beliefs about life after death*.

Explain
This means 'show that you understand something'. For example, *Explain different Jewish attitudes towards divorce*. An 'explain' response will include some knowledge, but the best responses will give a range of ideas and reasons.

Why
This word is used as shorthand for 'explain'. Put the word 'explain' in front of it and you will know what to do. For example, *Why are there different Jewish attitudes towards divorce?* is the same as *Explain why there are different Jewish attitudes towards divorce*.

How
This can be used to ask you for factual information. For example, *How do marriage ceremonies reflect Jewish teaching?* It can also be used for questions that are asking for understanding where there is a mixture of fact and understanding required.

Important
This word is used frequently in AO1 part d questions and it indicates that you need to say why someone should or should not do/believe something. An example is, *Explain why the Genesis creation stories are important to Jews*, which means, *Give reasons to explain why the Genesis creation stories are thought of as special in Judaism*.

Planning and structuring an answer

In the Grade Studios you have been shown how to build levels of response. This is really important for the AO1 responses to part d worth six marks and the AO2 responses to part e worth 12 marks. In each case follow this structure:

- Check you really know what the question is asking. In the AO2 questions work out the key word or words in the statement, for example *Sacred books are too old to be useful today. Discuss this statement*. The key phrase here is *Discuss this statement*. If the answer does not deal with this then it will be awarded a low mark.

- Make a note of key points to include all AO1 responses and use a diagram to note down viewpoints for AO2.

- Begin your answer with a brief mention of what the question is asking you to do.

- Write clearly and concisely. DON'T WAFFLE.

- Reach a conclusion at the end of your answer. In the case of an AO1 answer this could be a brief summary sentence, for example *So for these reasons Jews might want to help the poor.* In the case of an AO2 answer the conclusion should include a **personal view** (with supporting reasons/argument) and a **brief summing up** of the different views which you have expressed.

- Leave a gap of a few lines between each answer. This is in case you wish to add further ideas/information later (if you don't there is no need to worry).

- If you have any time left at the end of your exam, use it constructively. Check your answer makes sense. Check your answer is responding to the question set. Check your use of English, grammar and spelling. Check you have answered the required number of questions. **Remember, when you hand in your answer paper at the end of the exam it is probably the last time you will ever see it. Make sure it is your best possible effort.**

Glossary

anti-Semitic Speaking or acting against Jews.

Aramaic The original language of large sections of the books of Daniel and Ezra, and the main language of the Talmud.

Aron Hakodesh The focal point of the synagogue, containing Torah scrolls.

Ashkenazim Jews of Central and Eastern European origin.

Bar Mitzvah A boy's coming of age at 13 years old, usually marked by a synagogue ceremony and family celebration.

Bat Chayil Daughter of valour.

Bat Mitzvah A girl's coming of age at 12 years old. May be marked differently in different communities.

belief Something held to be true.

Bet ha knesset House of assembly.

Bet ha midrash House of study.

Bet ha tefilla House of prayer.

bimah Raised platform primarily for reading the Torah in the synagogue.

Brit Milah Circumcision. It is a sign of the relationship between G-d and humanity.

chazan or cantor Leader of reading, singing and chanting in the services of some synagogues.

covenant G-d's promise to help the people of Israel.

diaspora Jews living outside of the Jewish State of Israel.

faith Trust, confidence in and commitment to something or someone.

Gemara Commentary on the Mishnah included in the Talmud.

Gentile Person who is not Jewish.

Haftarah Passages from Nevi'im (Prophets) read in the synagogue (linked to weekly Torah and festival readings).

Hagadah A book used at Seder.

Halakhah Hebrew for 'walking with G-d'; putting Jewish beliefs into practice, living a Jewish life.

Hasidism A religious and social movement formed by Israel Baal Shem Tov (from the 18th century onwards).

Havdalah Ceremony marking the conclusion of Shabbat.

Holocaust The suffering experienced by European Jews at the hands of the Nazis, including the systematic murder of six million Jews between 1933 and 1945. Often called the Shoah.

holy Sacred; morally and spiritually perfect; separate from contamination and to be shown reverence.

huppah Canopy used for a wedding ceremony, under which the bride and groom stand.

Judaism The religion of the Jews.

Kabbalah Jewish mysticism.

Kaddish Prayer publicly recited by mourners.

kashru Means 'pure' and refers to food and other items that are acceptable to Jewish law.

kashrut Means 'pure'. Laws relating to keeping a kosher home and lifestyle.

Ketubah A Jewish document that defines rights and obligations within Jewish marriage.

Ketuvim Writings. Third section of the Tenakh.

Kibbutz Israeli collective village based on socialist principles.

Kiddush A prayer sanctifying Shabbat and festival days, usually recited over wine.

Kiddushin A Hebrew word applied to marriage, it means 'holy'.

Kippah, Yamulkah or Capel. Head covering worn during prayers, Torah study, etc. Some followers wear it constantly.

kittel Plain white robe worn by Jewish men, particularly on Yom Kippur.

kosher Foods permitted by Jewish dietary laws.

Magen David Star of David.

menorah Seven-branched candelabrum which was lit daily in the Temple.

Messiah A leader or deliverer sent by G-d to bring in a Messianic Age of peace.

mezuzah A scroll placed on doorposts of Jewish homes, containing a section from the Torah and often enclosed in a decorative case.

Midrash Collections of various Rabbinic commentaries on the Tenakh.

minyan Quorum of ten men, over Bar Mitzvah age, required for a service. Progressive communities may include women but do not always require a minyan.

Mishnah First writing down of the Oral Tradition. An authoritative document forming part of the Talmud, codified about 200 CE.

Mitzvah Commandment. The Torah contains 613 mitzvot.

mitzvot Commandments. The Torah contains 613 mitzvot.

Mohel Person trained to perform Brit Milah.

monotheist A person who believes in one G-d.

Muktzeh Objects that cannot be used on Shabbat.

Ner Tamid Eternal light. The perpetual light above the Aron Hakodesh.

Nevi'im Prophets. Second section of the Tenakh.

omnipotent G-d is all powerful.

omnipresent G-d is everywhere and at all times.

patriarchs The father and ruler of a family or tribe, in particular, Abraham, Isaac and Jacob.

Pesach Festival commemorating the Exodus from Egypt. One of the three biblical pilgrim festivals. Pesach is celebrated in the spring.

Pogrom Organised attack on Jews, especially frequent in 19th- and early 20th-century Eastern Europe.

rabbi A Jewish teacher. Often the religious leader of a Jewish community.

religion System of belief and practice – way of life built on belief in the divine (G-d).

rite of passage Ceremony to mark an important part of life such as birth or marriage.

Rosh Hashanah Jewish New Year.

Seder A home-based ceremonial meal during Pesach, at which the Exodus from Egypt is recounted using the Hagadah.

Sefer Torah Torah scroll. The five books of Moses handwritten on parchment and rolled to form a scroll.

Sephardim Jews originating from Mediterranean countries, especially Spain, North Africa and the Middle East.

Shabbat Day of spiritual renewal and rest commencing at sunset on Friday, terminating at nightfall on Saturday.

Shavuot One of three pilgrim festivals. Shavuot is celebrated in the summer, seven weeks after Pesach.

Shema A Jewish prayer affirming belief in one G-d. It is found in the Torah.

Shiva Seven days of intense mourning following the burial of a close relation. During this period, all ordinary work is prohibited.

Shoah See Holocaust.

Shofar Ram's horn blown at the season of Rosh Hashanah.

Siddur Order. Daily prayer book.

Simchat Torah Rejoicing of the law. Festival celebrating the completion and recommencement of the cycle of the weekly Torah reading.

sukkah A temporary dwelling used during Sukkot.

Sukkot One of three biblical pilgrim festivals, Sukkot is celebrated in the autumn.

synagogue or shul Building for Jewish public prayer, study and assembly.

tallit Prayer shawl. Four-cornered garment with fringes.

Talmud Mishnah (first writing down of the Oral Tradition) and Gemara (commentary on the Mishnah included in the Talmud), collected together.

Tefillah Self-judgement. Jewish prayer and meditation.

Tefillin Small leather boxes containing passages from the Torah, strapped on the forehead and arm for morning prayers on weekdays.

Tenakh The collected 35 books of the Jewish Bible, comprising three sections: Torah, Nevi'im, and Ketuvim (Te;Na;Kh).

Torah Law or teaching. The five Books of Moses in the Scriptures.

transcendent G-d is beyond the physical/natural world.

tzizit Fringes on the corners of the tallit. Also commonly refers to the fringed undervest worn by some Jewish males.

Yad Hand-held pointer used in reading the Sefer Torah.

Yishuv The Jewish community in Israel.

Yom Kippur Fast day occurring on the tenth day after Rosh Hashanah; a solemn day of Tefillah and Teshuva.

Zionism (Zion) Political movement securing the Jewish return to the Land of Israel.

Index